D0764589
井上雄彦

Takehiko Inoue

WHEN I WENT TO GO WATCH SUMO THE OTHER DAY, I WAS SUDDENLY OVERCOME BY THAT "WHOA" FEELING—THE KIND YOU GET WALKING INTO AN ARENA AT THE START OF A BASKETBALL GAME. THERE'S A UNIQUE "THICK" AIR AT THE KOKUGIKAN ARENA—THE KIND OF AIR THAT SLOWLY BUILDS WITH EACH GAME THAT'S PLAYED THERE, FROM WHEN THE SPORT WAS BORN UNTIL THE LATEST TIP-OFF. I NEVER FELT THAT AIR IN JAPAN UNTIL I FELT IT AT THE KOKUGIKAN. IT WAS THRILLING.

Takehiko Inoue's *Slam Dunk* is one of the most popular manga of all time, having sold over 100 million copies worldwide. He followed that series up with two titles lauded by critics and fans alike—*Vagabond*, a fictional account of the life of Miyamoto Musashi, and *Real*, a manga about wheelchair basketball.

SLAM DUNK
Vol. 23: A Rank vs. C Rank

SHONEN JUMP Manga Edition

STORY AND ART BY TAKEHIKO INOUE

English Adaptation/Stan!
Translation/Joe Yamazaki
Touch-up Art & Lettering/James Gaubatz
Cover & Graphic Design/Matt Hinrichs
Editor/Mike Montesa

Printed in the U.S.A.

Published by VIZ Media, LLC
P.O. Box 77010
San Francisco, CA 94107

10 9 8 7 6 5 4 3 2 1
First printing, August 2012

viz
media
www.viz.com

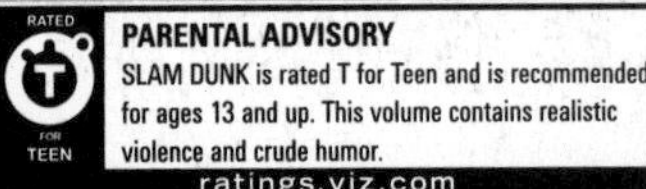
RATED
T
FOR
TEEN
PARENTAL ADVISORY
SLAM DUNK is rated T for Teen and is recommended for ages 13 and up. This volume contains realistic violence and crude humor.
ratings.viz.com

THE WORLD'S
MOST POPULAR MANGA
SHONEN
JUMP
www.shonenjump.com

SLAM DUNK
Vol. 23: A Rank vs. C Rank
STORY AND ART BY TAKEHIKO INOUE

Character Introduction

Hanamichi Sakuragi
A first-year at Shohoku High School, Sakuragi is in love with Haruko Akagi.

Haruko Akagi
Also a first-year at Shohoku, Takenori Akagi's little sister has a crush on Kaede Rukawa.

Takenori Akagi
A third-year and the basketball team's captain, Akagi has an intense passion for his sport.

Kaede Rukawa
The object of Haruko's affection (and that of many of Shohoku's female students!), this first-year has been a star player since junior high.

Coach Anzai
Shohoku High School Basketball Coach

Ryota Miyagi
A problem child with a thing for Ayako.

Hisashi Mitsui
An MVP during junior high.

Ayako
Basketball Team Manager

Our Story Thus Far

Hanamichi Sakuragi is rejected by close to 50 girls during his three years in junior high. He joins the basketball team to be closer to Haruko Akagi, but his frustration mounts when all he does is practice day after day.

Shohoku advances through the prefectural tournament to face Kainan University, but loses by two points.

Kainan defeats Ryonan in overtime in the second round to advance to the Nationals. On a dunk by Sakuragi with eight seconds remaining, Shohoku wins a tight game against Ryonan for the final remaining berth in the National Tournament.

Sakuragi's training for the Nationals begins.

Vol. 23: A Rank vs. C Rank

Table of Contents

#198	Shinkansen	7
#199	The Eve of the First Game	27
#200	A Rank Toyotama – C Rank Shohoku	47
#201	A Rank vs. C Rank	67
#202	Angry Phenom	87
#203	Gori on a Roll	107
#204	Jump Shot	127
#205	The Alleged Ace Killer	147
#206	We Are Beginners	167

SLAM DUNK
#198
SHINKANSEN

PNK
HMM ...?

READ
THIS
WAY

DONK
HMM...

...IT'S ACTUALLY KINDA HARD.
I CAN'T GET IT TO GO IN AT ALL.

WHAT'RE YOU DOING HERE, YOHEI?!
HUH ?

I HEARD NOISES, BUT EVERY-BODY'S AT THE NATIONALS ...

HEY, HARUKO.
I LEFT MY T-SHIRT...
...in the locker room when we slept over.

THE GYM'S QUIET WHEN ITS GUARDIANS AREN'T HERE.
PAA...
IT ECHOES A LOT IN HERE.
IT DOES.

IT MAY SOUND WEIRD, BUT THAT'S HOW I FEEL.
HANAMICHI WAS ABLE TO MAKE 20,000 SHOTS BECAUSE YOU GUYS STUCK WITH HIM TILL THE END.
WE OWE YOU ONE.
...

READ THIS WAY

HEH HEH ...
SO, AS SOMEONE WITH EXPERIENCE, HOW DOES HE LOOK?
IS HE REALLY IMPROV-ING?

HE'S AMAZING! HE SOAKED UP EVERYTHING COACH ANZAI TAUGHT HIM.
IF A NORMAL PERSON IS LIKE A LOCAL TRAIN...

...THEN HANAMICHI IS LIKE THE SHINKANSEN.
I'M SO JEAL-OUS.
WHSSH
HA HA HA

...

THAT ONE-HANDED SHOT THEY TAKE IS SO COOL.
I REALLY WANTED TO DO IT, TOO. I PRACTICED SO HARD.
I MADE TAKE-NORI TEACH ME.

OH, YEAH! GIRLS SHOOT TWO-HANDED, HUH?
Usually.
YEAH ...

I PRACTICED ALL THE TIME...
...ALL THROUGH JUNIOR HIGH.

I REMEMBER YOU PRACTICING DURING LUNCH.
YEAH.

BUT ...

FWP

SHWUH

BDNN

THREE YEARS OF PRACTICE AND THAT'S IT.
GRR
ARGH NGH GRR
I'm just ...
NOW, NOW.

IN JUST A WEEK HANA-MICHI... NO...
...IN A DAY, HE WENT RIGHT PAST ME.

I'M A BIT...
... JEALOUS. Y'KNOW?

...

WELL EVERYONE'S GOT STRENGTHS AND WEAKNESSES.
YOU JUST AREN'T CUT OUT FOR BASKETBALL.
D'YA HAVE TO BE SO BLUNT ?!

HUFF
PUFF
DON'T YOU THINK I KNOW THAT?!
UH... SORRY.

OH, I SHOULD GO.
I GOT-TA GET TO WORK.

WHO'D'A THOUGHT THAT HANAMICHI WOULD BE A NATIONAL-LEVEL ATHLETE?

IT TURNS OUT BASKET-BALL...
...WAS JUST RIGHT FOR HANA-MICHI.

READ
THIS
WAY

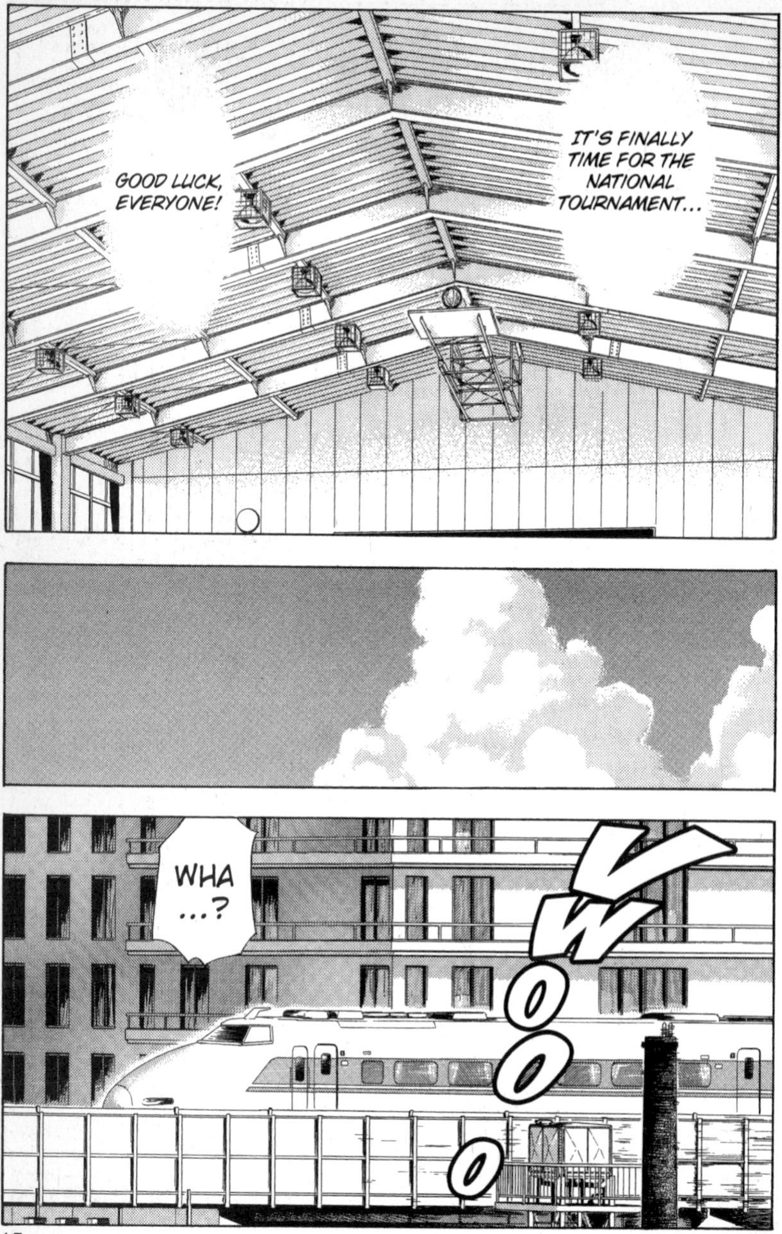

IT'S FINALLY TIME FOR THE NATIONAL TOURNAMENT...

GOOD LUCK, EVERYONE!

VWOOOO
WHA
...?

WHAT THE ...?!

Magazine: Weekly Basketball

S-SORRY, SIR.
STARE

...

山王工業(秋田)
湘北(神奈川)
豊玉(大阪)
熊本第三(熊本)
YO, THIS AIN'T FUNNY!
ARE THEY SERI-OUS?

WHAT? THIS TOYOTAMA TEAM IS THAT GOOD?
You rookie!
LOOK AT THE SECOND ROUND...

山王工業
YAMAOH...
NO, IT'S SAN-NOH.

Chart: Sanno Kogyo (Akita)
Shohoku (Kanagawa)
Toyotama (Osaka)
Kumamoto Dai San (Kumamoto)

READ THIS WAY

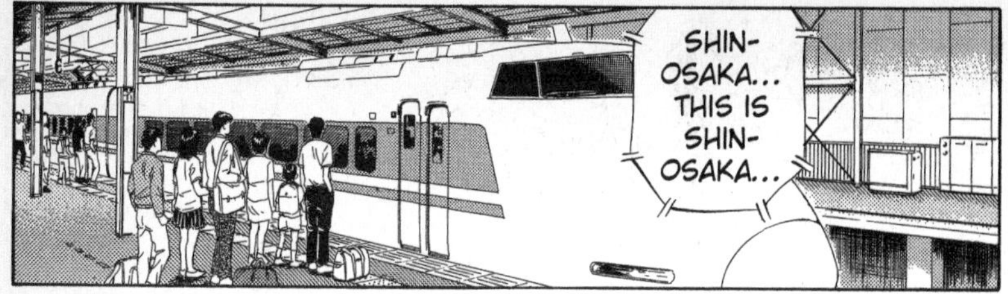
SHIN-OSAKA... THIS IS SHIN-OSAKA...

AKITA'S SANNOH KOGYO.
LAST YEAR'S CHAMPS.

THE CHAMPS ...!
NOT JUST LAST YEAR— TWO YEARS AGO, TOO...
...AND THE YEAR BEFORE THAT.

I'M GOING TO THE REST-ROOM...
COACH!

WHY DIDN'T YOU SHOW US THE DRAW?

...

I DIDN'T WANT THEM TO FEEL UNDUE PRESSURE ...
...OR RELIEF.

WE SHOULD BE WORRIED ABOUT HOW WE'RE PLAYING, NOT WHO WE'RE PLAYING.

...

AFTER WE BEAT YAMAOH, WHO DO WE PLAY IN THE THIRD ROUND?
IT'S SAN-NOH!
THIRD ROUND ...?

山王工業(秋田)
Sannoh Kogyo (Akita)
湘 北(神奈川)
Shohoku (Kanagawa)
豊 玉(大阪)
Toyotama (Osaka)
熊本第三(熊本)
Kumamoto Dai-San (Kumamoto)
北条四商(福岡)
Hojo Yon-Sho (Fukuoka)
横玉工業(兵庫)
Yokotama Kogyo (Hyogo)
愛和学院(愛知)
Aiwa Gakuin (Aichi)
OH, WHOA... IT'S AIWA GAKUIN!
YOU'RE KIDDIN' ME!
THEY WERE IN THE FINAL FOUR LAST YEAR!
HMM... AICHI'S STAR, HUH?
YOU KNOW HIM?
THEY CARRIED HIM OFF ON A STRETCHER. NO BIGGIE.
OH?

READ THIS WAY

OH.
MY BAD!
...!!

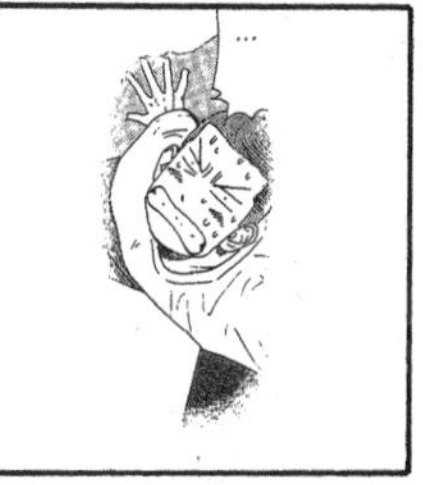
...

...
商
名朋工

IN THE OPPO-SITE BRACKET.
TSK
I'LL BE SEEING HIM IN THE FINALS!

Chart: Shogyo
Meiho Kogyo

SANNOH KOGYO AND AIWA GAKUIN...

WE'RE IN A TOUGH BRACKET!

SHWFF

?!

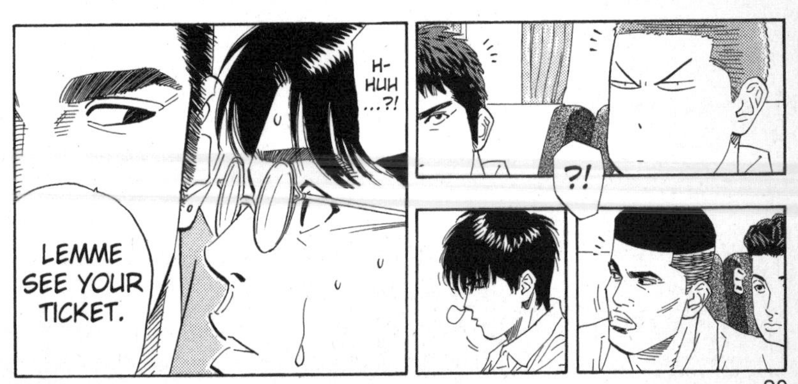

LEMME SEE YOUR TICKET.
H-HUH...?!
?!

SHIN-YOKO-HAMA TO HIRO-SHIMA...
HEY...

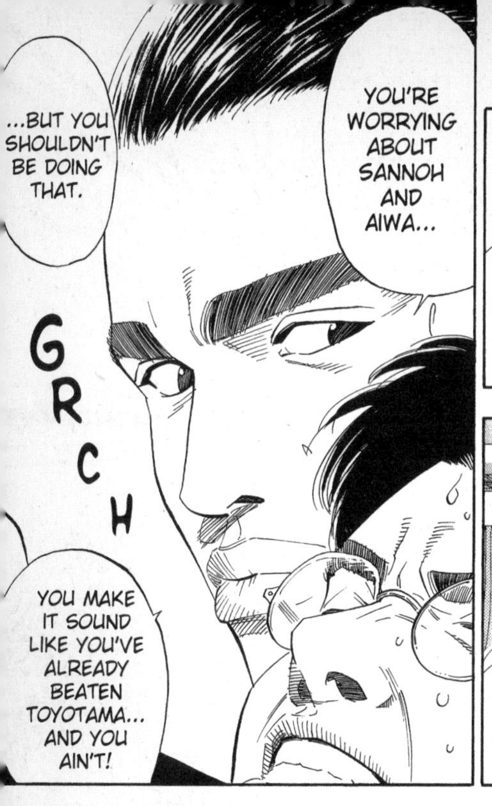
YOU'RE WORRYING ABOUT SANNOH AND AIWA...
...BUT YOU SHOULDN'T BE DOING THAT.
GRCH
YOU MAKE IT SOUND LIKE YOU'VE ALREADY BEATEN TOYOTAMA... AND YOU AIN'T!

HEY !!
SKF
WHO ARE YOU?!

W-What's going on?
...!
GRRCH
YOU PUNKS GOTTA BE SHOHOKU.
...

TOYO-
TAMA
...?
SHF

HEY! STOP THAT, KISHI-MOTO!
WHAT'RE YOU DOING?!

HMPH
...

I-I'M SORRY, BOYS! ARE YOU HURT?
WHY YOU APOLO-GIZING, COACH?
THESE GUYS WERE TALKING TRASH ABOUT US.

JERK! WHY WOULD WE EVEN THINK ABOUT YOU?

WHO DO YOU THINK YOU'RE TALKING TO, SCRUB?
LOOK AT THE MAGAZINE, FOOL!
STOP IT, KISH-IMOTO!! LET'S GO!!

READ THIS WAY

C 湘

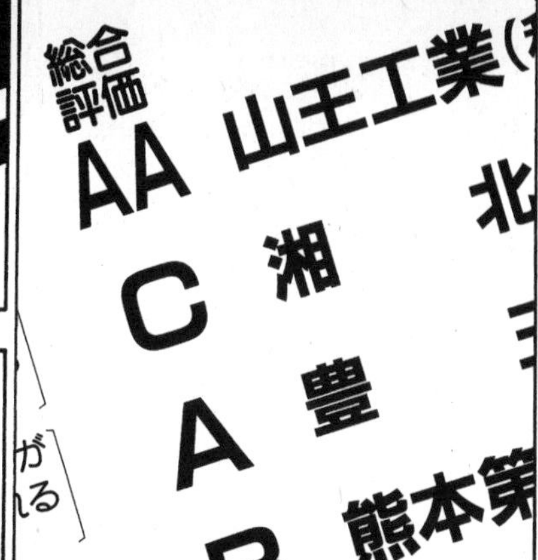
総合評価
AA 山王工業(
C 湘 北
A 豊
B 熊本第
が
れる

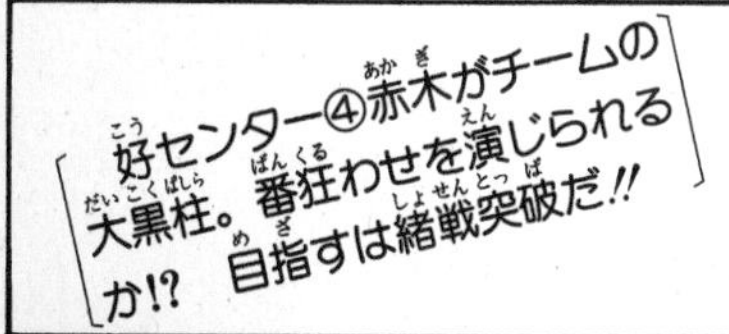
好センター④赤木がチームの大黒柱。番狂わせを演じられるか!?
目指すは緒戦突破だ!!

Article: [Skilled center (4) Akagi is the team's leader. Will they be able to pull off an upset? Their first goal is to win the opening round!]

HMPH
THEY THINK THEY'RE GONNA PLAY SANNOH!
CLUELESS IDIOTS!

Chart: Overall Rank
AA Sannoh Kogyo (Akita)
C Shohoku
A Toyotama
B Kumamoto Dai...

TH
UD
?!
...
SH
F
YA
NK
HEY!!
HMM?
HMMM

READ THIS WAY

STOP IT, KISHI-MOTO!! LET GO!!
TMP TMP
LET HIM GO!
I-IS THERE A PROB-LEM?

C'MON!!

HEY, TOP-KNOT.

HUH?!

DON'T FORGET, YOU GRABBED MY HEAD.
THE FIRST ROUND'S GONNA BE A WAR.
Oh no!

Hiroshima...
Hiroshima...
GASP
SKSSH
SLAM DUNK

THE EVE OF THE FIRST GAME

THE SUMMER CHAMPIONSHIPS.
THE AUTUMN NATIONAL SPORTS FESTIVAL.
THE WINTER INVITATIONAL.
総合体育大会
広島駅 HIROSHIMA STATION
THE THREE GREAT TOURNAMENTS OF HIGH SCHOOL BASKETBALL.
歓 全国高校総体 迎
広島市高等学校推進委員会

Sign: Welcome
National High School Championships
Hiroshima City High School Committee

SUMMER, HIRO-SHIMA ...

WE, THE ATHLETES ...

READ THIS WAY

#199 THE EVE OF THE FIRST GAME

全国高校総体
... HEREBY SWEAR TO ...

THE THREE GREAT HIGH SCHOOL TOURNA-MENTS...

全国高校総体
年8月1日
Sign: Welcome to Hiroshima National High School Championships August 1st

Sign: Welcome to Hiroshima

歓迎
歓迎
Sign: Welcome Welcome

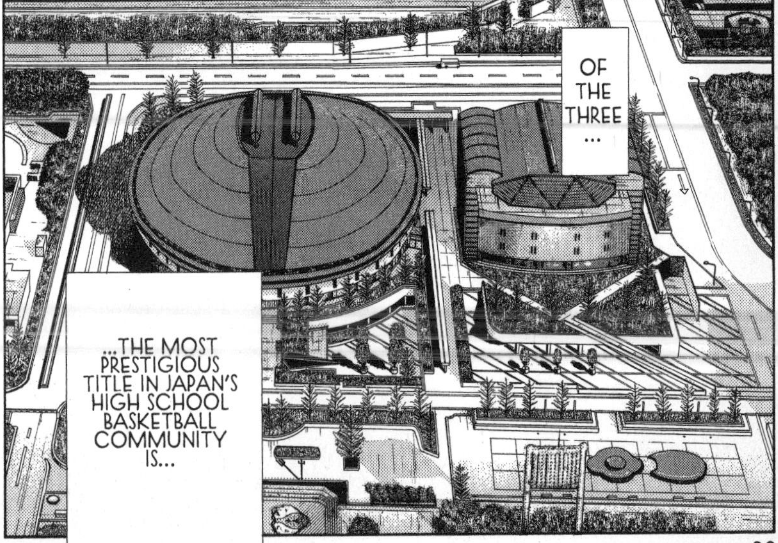
OF THE THREE ...
...THE MOST PRESTIGIOUS TITLE IN JAPAN'S HIGH SCHOOL BASKETBALL COMMUNITY IS...

READ
THIS
WAY

WINNING THE NATIONALS.
BUNN
NATIONAL HIGH SC KETBA
MEN'S TOURNAME

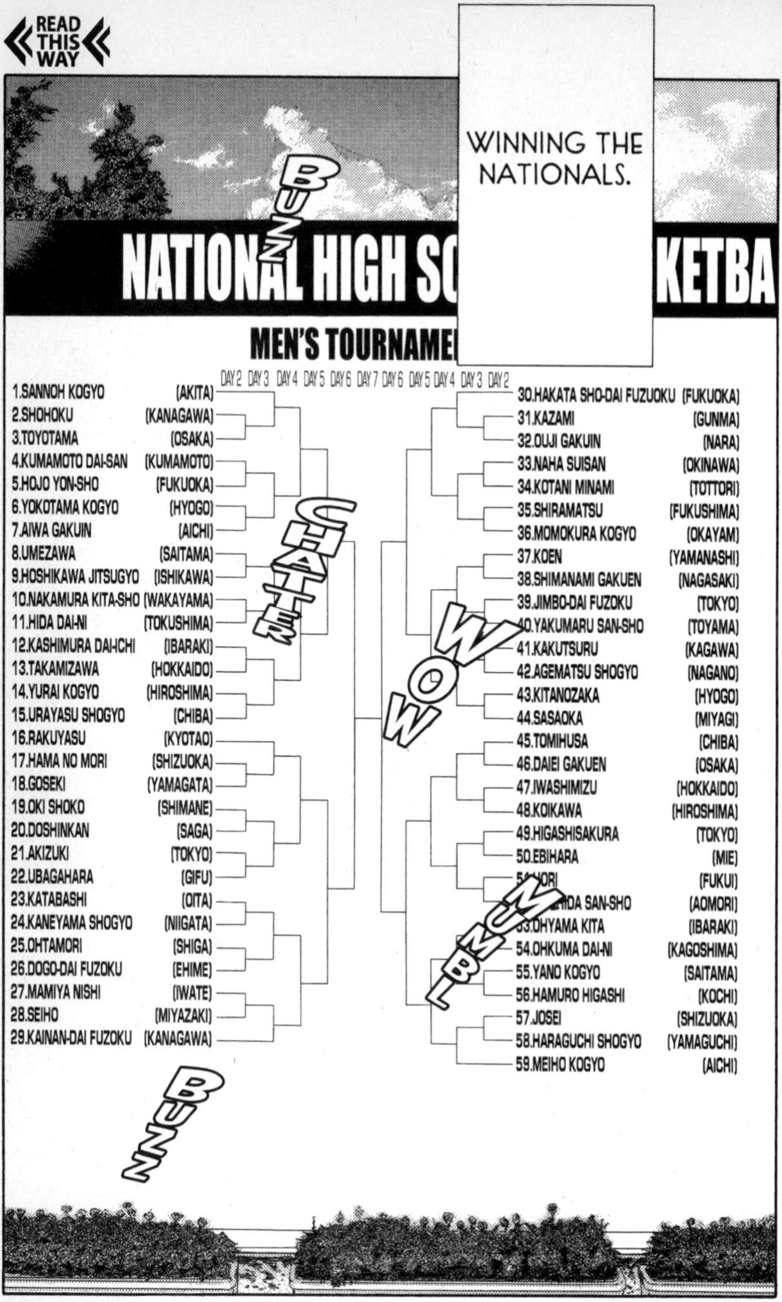

DAY 2 DAY 3 DAY 4 DAY 5 DAY 6 DAY 7 DAY 6 DAY 5 DAY 4 DAY 3 DAY 2

Team	Prefecture	Team	Prefecture
1.SANNOH KOGYO	(AKITA)	30.HAKATA SHO-DAI FUZUOKU	(FUKUOKA)
2.SHOHOKU	(KANAGAWA)	31.KAZAMI	(GUNMA)
3.TOYOTAMA	(OSAKA)	32.OUJI GAKUIN	(NARA)
4.KUMAMOTO DAI-SAN	(KUMAMOTO)	33.NAHA SUISAN	(OKINAWA)
5.HOJO YON-SHO	(FUKUOKA)	34.KOTANI MINAMI	(TOTTORI)
6.YOKOTAMA KOGYO	(HYOGO)	35.SHIRAMATSU	(FUKUSHIMA)
7.AIWA GAKUIN	(AICHI)	36.MOMOKURA KOGYO	(OKAYAM)
8.UMEZAWA	(SAITAMA)	37.KOEN	(YAMANASHI)
9.HOSHIKAWA JITSUGYO	(ISHIKAWA)	38.SHIMANAMI GAKUEN	(NAGASAKI)
10.NAKAMURA KITA-SHO	(WAKAYAMA)	39.JIMBO-DAI FUZOKU	(TOKYO)
11.HIDA DAI-NI	(TOKUSHIMA)	40.YAKUMARU SAN-SHO	(TOYAMA)
12.KASHIMURA DAI-ICHI	(IBARAKI)	41.KAKUTSURU	(KAGAWA)
13.TAKAMIZAWA	(HOKKAIDO)	42.AGEMATSU SHOGYO	(NAGANO)
14.YURAI KOGYO	(HIROSHIMA)	43.KITANOZAKA	(HYOGO)
15.URAYASU SHOGYO	(CHIBA)	44.SASAOKA	(MIYAGI)
16.RAKUYASU	(KYOTAO)	45.TOMIHUSA	(CHIBA)
17.HAMA NO MORI	(SHIZUOKA)	46.DAIEI GAKUEN	(OSAKA)
18.GOSEKI	(YAMAGATA)	47.IWASHIMIZU	(HOKKAIDO)
19.OKI SHOKO	(SHIMANE)	48.KOIKAWA	(HIROSHIMA)
20.DOSHINKAN	(SAGA)	49.HIGASHISAKURA	(TOKYO)
21.AKIZUKI	(TOKYO)	50.EBIHARA	(MIE)
22.UBAGAHARA	(GIFU)	5 ORI	(FUKUI)
23.KATABASHI	(OITA)	IDA SAN-SHO	(AOMORI)
24.KANEYAMA SHOGYO	(NIIGATA)	3.OHYAMA KITA	(IBARAKI)
25.OHTAMORI	(SHIGA)	54.OHKUMA DAI-NI	(KAGOSHIMA)
26.DOGO-DAI FUZOKU	(EHIME)	55.YANO KOGYO	(SAITAMA)
27.MAMIYA NISHI	(IWATE)	56.HAMURO HIGASHI	(KOCHI)
28.SEIHO	(MIYAZAKI)	57.JOSEI	(SHIZUOKA)
29.KAINAN-DAI FUZOKU	(KANAGAWA)	58.HARAGUCHI SHOGYO	(YAMAGUCHI)
		59.MEIHO KOGYO	(AICHI)

CHATTER

WOW

MUMBL

BUNN

HMM
HMPH
MUMBLE
YEAH
MY CONDO-LENCES.

WHA?

CHING
IN THE SAME BLOCK AS SANNOH AND AIWA.
That's rough.

YOU GUYS ARE TOAST.
SNORK
GRR
WHAT'D YOU SAY, YOU WILD MON-KEY?

LOOKS LIKE YOU AND I WON'T BE HAVING A REMATCH, RUKAWA.

I WAS HOPING WE COULD SETTLE IT HERE.
Settle?
...

SANNOH AND AIWA... BWA HA HA!

READ THIS WAY

WE'VE GOTTA BEAT THEM EVENTUALLY, TOO.
IT'S JUST A MATTER OF TIME.

MMM ...

EXACTLY.

WE HAVE TO CRUSH ALL THE OTHER TEAMS TO WIN THE TITLE!

WE'LL SEE YOU GUYS IN THE SEMIS, MAKI.
HEH
HOPE SO. THAT'D BE GOOD FOR US.
1階

HAR HAR HAR!! SURE WOULD BE!!
Good one, Maki!

BONK
...
D'OH ?!

WE WON'T LOSE TO YOU A SECOND TIME!!
PLAY HARD!!

SMIRK
YOU GUYS, TOO.

WHOA, WHOA, WHOA! YOU GUYS CAN'T BE SERIOUS!
YOU PLANNING TO PLAY KAINAN?!

HMM ?!

WHAT'RE YOU FOOLS THINKING?
TMP
TOYOTAMA

READ
THIS
WAY

OH.
YOU
PUNKS.
FOR-
GET IT.
LET'S
GO.

YO, MAKI!
I HEARD YOU
STRUGGLED
AGAINST
THESE GUYS
IN THE
REGIONALS.
HOW'D
THAT
HAP-
PEN?

GUESS THAT
MEANS YOUR
SPOT IN THE
FINAL FOUR IS
UP FOR GRABS.

...!!

...

SORRY.
WHO
ARE
YOU
AGAIN?
...!!

HA HA HA HA
BWA HA HA HA HA HA!!
NICE!!
ACTING LIKE A BIG SHOT!! YOU'RE STILL TEN YEARS AWAY FROM TALKING TO MAKI LIKE THAT!!

SKF
YOU WANT SOME? HUH?!
WE'LL KILL YOU!!

TOPKNOT!!
GRRRR
...

SKF
OH? YOU GUYS WANNA GO?

HEY! WHAT'S GOING ON?
HEY
WHAP
A FIGHT?
HUH

READ THIS WAY

KNOCK IT OFF !!

PHEW!

STOP THIS NON-SENSE !!
HRRM.

HE'S RIGHT. BACK OFF, KISHI-MOTO.
KISHIMOTO
YAJIMA

...!!

I'M PRETTY SURE THAT'S TOYOTAMA'S CAPTAIN, MINAMI.
He's smooth.
I remember him...
...!!

RUKAWA, WATCH OUT FOR HIM.

...

TOMORROW WE'LL FIND OUT WHO'S BETTER.

AKAGI, WE'RE BASKET-BALL PLAYERS.
WIN OR LOSE, NO HARD FEELINGS.
TOYOTAMA

DAMN RIGHT.

SKF
LET'S GO!
MINAMI
KISHIMOTO

READ THIS WAY

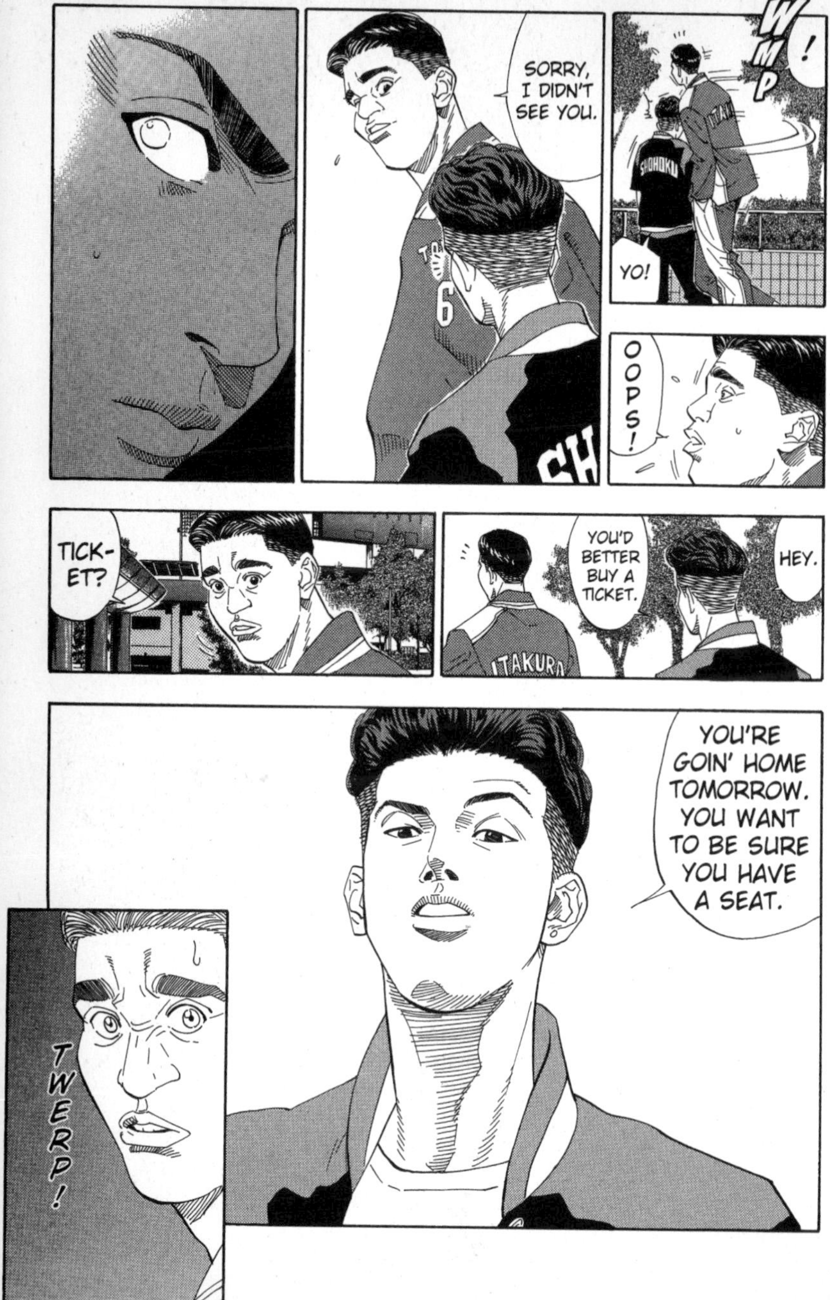

WMP
!
YO!

OOPS!

SORRY, I DIDN'T SEE YOU.

HEY.
YOU'D BETTER BUY A TICKET.

TICK-ET?

YOU'RE GOIN' HOME TOMORROW. YOU WANT TO BE SURE YOU HAVE A SEAT.

TWERP!

...

Sign: Hiroshima Chidoriso Inn

A PUNK SINCE CHILDHOOD ... ♪

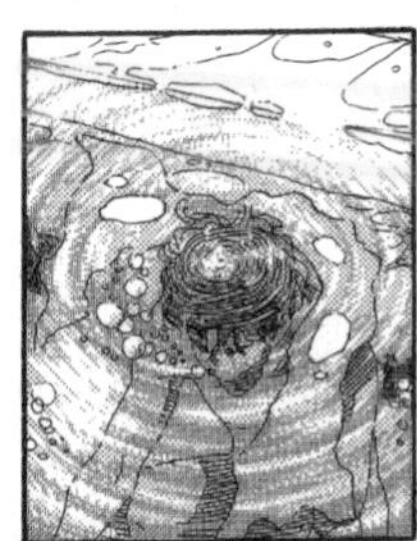

SPOOSH

...
I DIDN'T SEE YOU.

READ THIS WAY

SPLASH

FUNNY-FACE...
...I'M GONNA CRUSH YOU TOMORROW.

竹の間

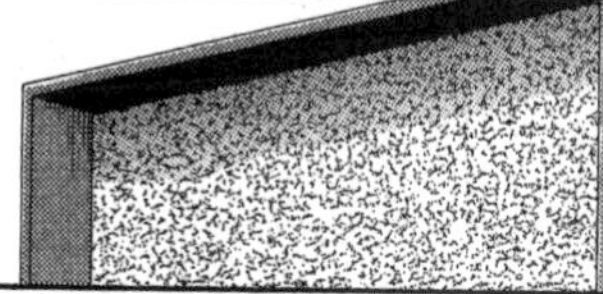

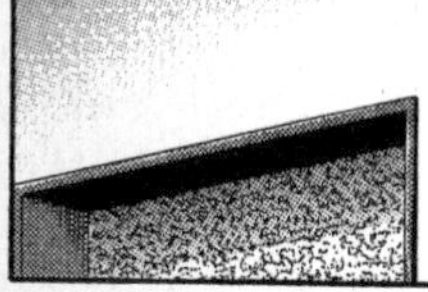

Sign: *Take no Ma* (Bamboo room/suite)

VISUALIZATION TRAINING
I'M THE BEST IN JAPAN, I'M THE BEST IN JAPAN, I'M THE BEST IN JAPAN...

FELL ASLEEP
ZZZ

TH-TH-TH-THAT'S RIGHT, HARUKO!
HA HA HA!
I HOPE YOUR TRAINING CAMP PAYS OFF.

U-UM...
DMP
BDMP
TOMORROW...
YES...?
...
GULP
I'M GONNA SAY IT.
...
T-TOMORROW, HARUKO, BECAUSE... ♡
DONK
SLIP
OOPS!
...I LUV YA...
...I'M GOING TO PLAY MY VERY BEST!!
THAT'S GREAT. GOOD LUCK.

ちどり荘
Sign: Chidoriso

OUR FIRST GAME'S TOMORROW.
GET SOME REST.
RIGHT!!

READ
THIS
WAY

WHAT'S UP WITH THIS MAGAZINE?!
HMPH
HARUMPH

WHY ARE WE A C RANK?

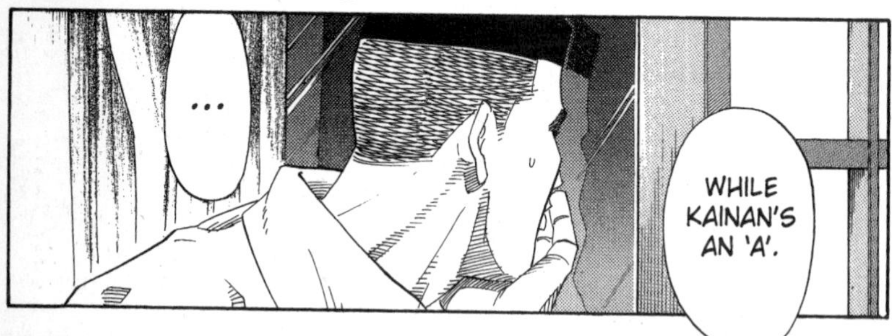
WHILE KAINAN'S AN 'A'.
...

TOYO-TAMA'S AN 'A'? THAT CAN'T BE RIGHT!
HMPH

AKAGI ...
YOU ALL RIGHT?

HUH ?

MITSUI ...
DID YOU GET NERVOUS IN JUNIOR HIGH?

AT THE JUNIOR NATION-ALS?
I DON'T REMEM-BER.

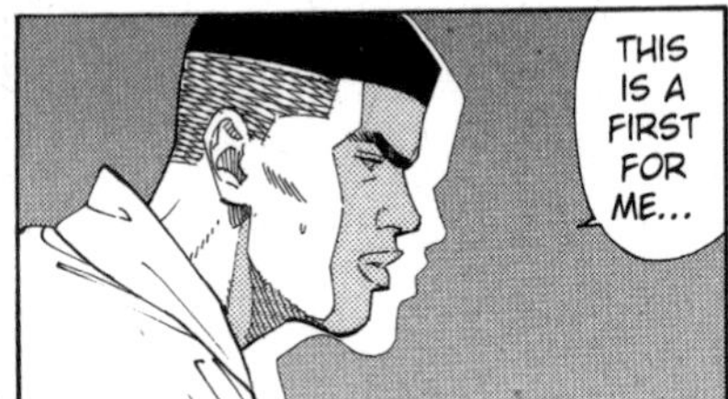
THIS IS A FIRST FOR ME...

I CAN'T STOP SHAKING.

I'M GOING FOR A RUN.
TNK

EVEN HE GETS NERVOUS, HUH?
I DON'T BLAME HIM.

HE'S DREAMED OF PLAYING IN THE NATIONALS SINCE ELEMENTARY SCHOOL.

TMP
TMP

WE CAN'T LOSE TOMORROW.

HF HF HF

Excuse me. Which way is Chidoriso?
I'm lost.
YAH!
What the–?!
SLAM DUNK

#200

年度全国高等学校総合体
第　回全国高等学校バスケットボール選手

参加申込書

学校名	神奈川県立湘北高等学校
略称名	湘北高
監督氏名	安西光義
主将氏名	赤木剛憲

学校所在地
代表者氏名
コーチ
マネージャー

ユニフォームNo.	選手名	学年	生年月日	身長	出
4	赤木剛憲	3	.5.10	197cm	土
5	木暮公延	3	.7.12	178	北
6	安田靖春	2	.3.28	164	立
7	宮城リョータ	2	.7.31	168	立
8	潮崎哲士	2	.9.23	170	谷
9	角田悟	2	.11.4	180	谷
10	桜木花道	1	.4.1	188	和光
11	流川楓	1	.1.1	187	富ケ丘
12	石井健太郎	1	.1.18	170	大塚
13	佐々岡智	1	.10.13	171	大塚
14	三井寿	3	.5.22	184	武石中
15	桑田登紀	1	.7.28	162	藤園中

上記の者は本校在学生徒で標記大会に出場することを認め、参加申込みをいたします。

年 7月1日

高等学校長

上記 神奈川(都道府県)代表として標記大会に出

年 7月4日

A RANK TOYOTAMA — C RANK SHOHOKU

See page 66 for a translation of the form.

AUGUST 2ND
TWEET
CHIRP
HIRO-SHIMA
FINALLY THE FIRST ROUND OF THE NATIONALS IS HERE!
CHIRP CHIRP...
EVERYBODY HERE?
YES !!
HA HA HA
YOU WERE IN THE BATHROOM FOR A LONG TIME, GORI! DROP A LOAD SO BIG IT WOULDN'T FLUSH?!
Probably.
BONK
ACK!
GEEZ! D'YA HAFTA HIT ME RIGHT BEFORE I...
... MAKE MY DE-BUT?
HMPH MRPH
SHUT UP.
Moron!

READ THIS WAY

...

I CAN'T STOP SHAKING.

LOOKS LIKE AKAGI GOT OVER IT.
YUP. BACK TO HIS USUAL SELF.

EVERYBODY'S ACTUALLY KIND OF RELAXED.
HEH
YEAH

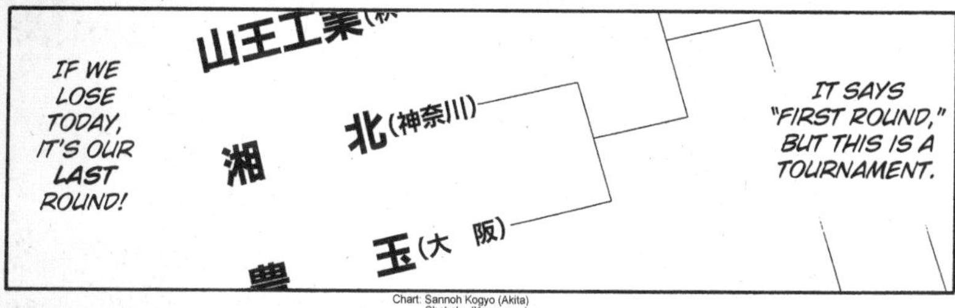
IT SAYS "FIRST ROUND," BUT THIS IS A TOURNAMENT.
山王工業(秋
湘 北(神奈川)
玉(大 阪)
IF WE LOSE TODAY, IT'S OUR LAST ROUND!

Chart: Sannoh Kogyo (Akita)
Shohoku (Kanagawa)
Toyotama (Osaka)

I'M NOT READY TO RETIRE TODAY!

LET'S GO!!

YEAH!!

OH, BOYS ...!

... THERE'S A PHONE CALL FOR YOU!
PHONE CALL?
WHO COULD THAT BE...?

SOMEONE NAMED HIKOICHI AIDA.

RYONAN'S HIKOICHI?!
WHY WOULD HE CALL?
Let's see.
OH, THAT NOISY FRESH-MAN?

THERE'S A FAX FOR YOU, TOO.
One big fax.
SHMF
?!

DID YOU GET THE FAX?

THAT'S MY DATA FROM THEIR OSAKA REGIONAL FINALS!
I THINK YOU'LL FIND IT PRETTY HELPFUL!

READ THIS WAY

㊙情報
あなただけに そっとおしえる…
これが豊玉だ!!
by 相田彦一
HMM...

Fax: Top Secret Info Just for you... How to Beat Toyotama! By Hikoichi Aida

IT'S THE LEAST I COULD DO!
'CUZ I REALLY WANT SHOHOKU TO WIN!

FOOL.
Kishimoto
IDIOT.
Teruo
FWOOSH
YOU BETTER NOT LOSE!!

RYONAN'S NOT COMING TO WATCH...
...THE PHENOM SAKURAGI'S NATIONAL DEBUT?
OH, SAKURAGI!

WELL ...
WE'RE PRACTICING TO BEAT SHOHOKU NEXT YEAR!

IS EVERYBODY THERE?
YEAH, WE'RE ALL HERE...

...
HEFF

GO! GO!

SHO-HO-KU!!!

SON

おいしさホットなお弁当

FLINCH

...
RNNNG
...
RNNNG

READ THIS WAY

THANKS, HIKOICHI. WE'LL WIN!
KOGU-RE?!
HOW CAN WE WIN IF OUR EAR DRUMS ARE RUPTURED ?!

I'LL BE CHEERING FROM KANA-GAWA!
CLK

HO HO. HERE WE GO!
STOMP
YEAH!!

GOOD LUCK, BOYS!
VROOO
BYE BYE!
YOU'RE GONNA FALL OUT, SAKURAGI!
PUSH HIM! PUSH HIM!

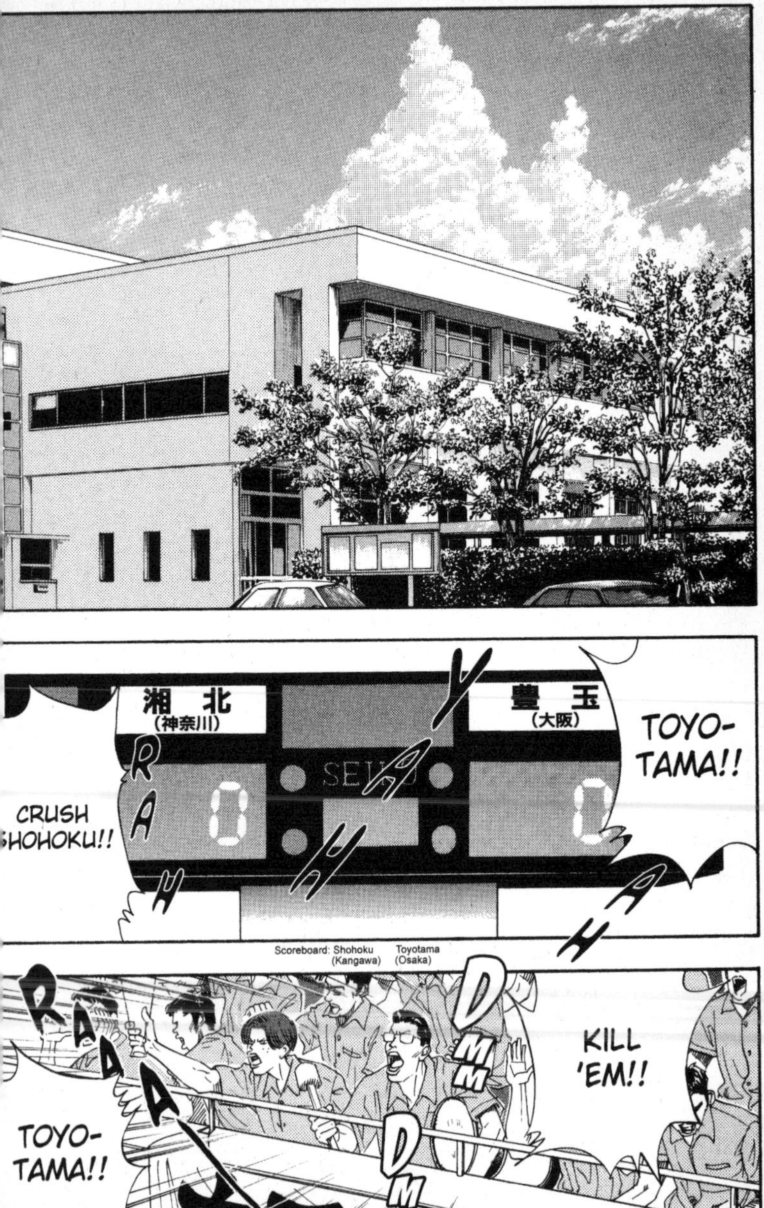

TOYO-TAMA!!

YAAHH

湘北
(神奈川)

豊玉
(大阪)

0

0

RAAH

CRUSH SHOHOKU!!

AAHH

Scoreboard: Shohoku (Kangawa) Toyotama (Osaka)

KILL 'EM!!

DMM

DMM

RAAAAAH

TOYO-TAMA!!

READ THIS WAY

Entrance banner: Welcome National High-School Championships
Entrance Sign: National High School Championship Boy's Basketball Ar

MRMR
BUZZ
BUZZ
I'M KINDA SCARED.
MAYBE WE PICKED...
...THE WRONG SECTION TO SIT IN, NORI?
RAAA
KILL 'EM
GRA
SH-SHUT UP!!
WHAT?!
KILL 'EM
THE BATTLE'S ALREADY STARTED! STOP BEING SUCH A WUSS!
WHAT D'YOU THINK WE CAME TO HIROSHIMA FOR?

URRAAH!!

!!

NORI!!

SHOHOKU!!

FWAP

FWAP

FWAP

Flag: Man on Fire
Mitsui

...!!

AIEEE! RUN, NORI! RUN!
HUH?

TMP TMP TMP TMP TMP
YOU PICKIN' A FIGHT WITH US?!
HEY!
STOP!
AAAH! RUN FOR YOUR LIVES!

CHAT
BUZZ
BUZZ
MRMR

豊玉高校
控 室

SHOHOKU MIGHT NOT BE WELL KNOWN, BUT THEY PUT UP A FIGHT AGAINST KAINAN!
THEY HAVE SERIOUS POTENTIAL! BE SHARP OUT THERE!

Sign: Toyotama High School Locker Room

...

"POTENTIAL"? WHAT DOES THAT MEAN?
C'MON, MAN, WE'RE A BUNCHA JOCKS.

IT MEANS THEY MIGHT REALLY BE GOOD.
THEY'RE A MYS-TERY.

THEIR SCORING LEADER'S A FRESHMAN, HUH?

TYPICAL FOR UPSTART SCHOOLS.
ANOTHER TEAM THAT GOT HERE ON THE BACK OF A BIG TIME ROOKIE?

HE'S PRETTY BIG. 187 CM.

HOW DO YOU READ THIS?
NAGARE-KAWA?

READ THIS WAY

THEN I'LL DEFEND NAGAREKAWA AT FIRST.

...
AT FIRST, HUH?

WATCH OUT FOR THEIR CENTER, AKAGI, TOO!
THERE'S A LOT OF TALK ABOUT HIM!

...
HMPH

...

湘北高校
控室

Sign: Shohoku High School Locker Room

I'LL WIN THE OPENING JUMP BALL!
RUKAWA, YOU TAKE OFF RUNNING!
WE'LL TRY TO SCORE A QUICK ONE LIKE WE DID AGAINST KAINAN.

GOT IT.
GORI, YOU SURE ABOUT HIM?
THE OLD MAN STOPPED HIM THAT GAME.
Utter failure.

SHUT UP!
NOBODY'S STOPPING ME TODAY.

SAKURAGI! SHOW US WHAT YOU LEARNED AT TRAINING CAMP.
I KNEW IT!
YOU HAVE BIG PLANS FOR ME.

...
GRIN

MY NATIONAL DEBUT.
BDMP...
I'M NOT THE SAME PLAYER I WAS AT THE REGIONALS.
BDMP...
BDMP...
A LOT HAPPENED THERE...
Like getting ejected.

READ
THIS
WAY

TODAY PHENOM SAKURAGI RECEIVES THE ATTENTION OF THE NATION!

BDMP...

BDMP...

BDMP...

SHF
...

COACH...
WHAT DO YOU THINK ABOUT US GETTING A C RANK?

C 湘 北(神奈
A 豊 玉(大

Chart: C Shohoku (Kanagawa)
A Toyotama (Osaka)

HO HO.
I THINK IT'S GREAT!

Magazine: Weekly Basketball

HUH...?

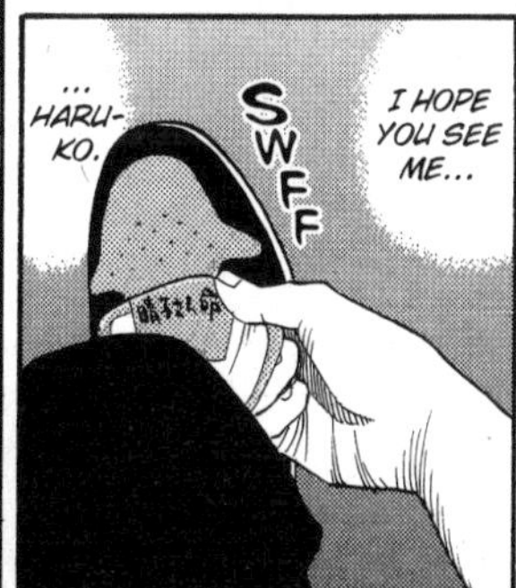
I HOPE YOU SEE ME...
SWFF
...HARUKO.

Tongue: Haruko Love

THERE'S NO PRESSURE ON US.
PAT
RIGHT NOW NOBODY THINKS WE CAN WIN.

AA 山王工業
C 湘 北
A 豊 玉
熊本第三(熊本)
(福岡)
THEY'LL KNOW DIFFERENT WHEN IT'S OVER.
IF THIS IS WHAT THEY THINK ABOUT US...

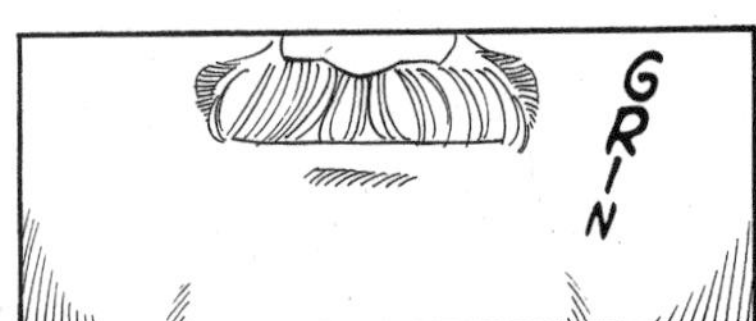
GRIN

...LET'S SHOW THEM HOW ***WRONG*** THEY ARE.

READ THIS WAY

OH YEAH ...

READY?

YES!!

SHOHOKU...

FIGHT!

YEAH!!

BAMMM
LET'S GO BEAT TOYOTAMA!!!
YEAH!!
SQUEAK

SQUEAK
SQUEAK
SQUEAK
SQUEAK
SQUEAK
SHOHOKU
SHOHOKU
SHOHOKU
SHOHOKU

... Year Inter-High School Championship
th/rd National High School Basketball Player...

Participation Application

School Name Kanagawa Prefecture Shohoku **High School** **School Location**
Abbreviated Name Shohoku High **Representative**
Head Coach Name Mitsuyoshi Anzai **Coach**
Captain Name Takenori Akagi **Manager**

Uniform No.	Player Name	Grade	Date of Birth	Height	Junior High School
4	Takenori Akagi	3	. 5 . 10	197 cm	Kitamura
5	Kiminobu Kogure	3	. 7 . 12	178	Kitamura
6	Yasuharu Yasuda	2	. 3 . 28	164	Tachi
7	Ryota Miyagi	2	. 7 . 31	168	Tachi
8	Tetsushi Shiozaki	2	. 9 . 23	170	Tani
9	Satoru Kakuta	2	. 11 . 4	180	Tani
10	Hanamichi Sakuragi	1	. 4 . 1	188	Wako
11	Kaede Rukawa	1	. 1 . 1	187	Tomigaoka
12	Kentaro Ishii	1	. 1 . 18	170	Ohtuska Ni
13	Satoru Sasaoka	1	. 10 . 13	171	Ohtsuka Ni
14	Hisashi Mitsui	3	. 5 . 22	184	Takeishi Jr.
15	Toki Kuwata	1	. 7 . 28	162	Fujizono Jr.

We acknowledge the persons above as enrolled students of our school and permit their participation in said tournament, and hereby submit our participation application.

Year 7 **Month** 1 **Day** Toshi Takanaga

As representative of above Kanagawa (To/Do/Fu/Ken), I hereby permit their participation in said tournament, and hereby submit our participation application.

Year 7 **Month** 4 **Day**
Kanagawa **(To/DoFu/Ken) High School Athletic Federation Chairman** Kantara Nantara

Year Inter-High School Championship Chairman Mr.

Entry fee of 15,000 yen will be deposited to with a deposit slip to the bank designated in the implementation guideline 9 (2)....

Excuse me, where's the entrance to the court?
We're lost.
Huh ?
SLAM DUNK

A RANK VS. C RANK

C'MON!
TOYOTAMA!
WOOOO!!
KILL 'EM!
DMM DMM DMM DMM

Banner: *Doryoku* (effort/hard work)
Toyotama High School Basketball

Sign: National High School Basketball

THEY'RE A REAL CLASSY CROWD.

THOSE TOYO-TAMA GUYS.

TWITCH

HEY!!

WHERE WERE YOU GUYS?!
SKF
HF
NORI?
Why you guys crying?
WE ALMOST GOT KILLED!

HERE THEY COME!
SHOHO-KU!

GO, SHO-HO-KU!!
YAY
SHOHOKU!!
RAH
ットボール選手権大会
JABBA
流川命
YAY
A RANK VS. C RANK

RAAAH! TOYO-TAMA!!
WOO
DMM DMM DMM DMM
RAH
WOH
努力
豊玉高等学校バスケット部
GO GET 'EM!!
TOYO-TAMA!!
#201

HEY! WHAT'S THAT?!
LOOKIT THAT WEIRDO!

...

HEY, YOU! NUMBER TEN!
WHAT'S WITH YOUR HAIR?!
HMM?
YOU GONNA PICK A FIGHT?
KISHIMOTO! KILL THAT NUMBER TEN! KILL HIM!
SHOHOKU
10

ROOAAAR
I PLAN TO. I DON'T NEED YOU GUYS TO TELL ME.

HAMANICHI'S ALREADY PUBLIC ENEMY NUMBER ONE!
WHA HEH
AHH
HOW COULD HE NOT BE?
HMM
WOH
IT'S THAT HAIR OF HIS!

YOU'RE AWFULLY POPULAR, HANAMICHI.
HEY, YOU!
HA HA HA HA.
PAA...
Don't worry about the heckling.
...

SO THEY WANNA PUT PRESSURE ON THE STAR BEFORE THE GAME, HUH?
I get it.
THE STAR? You?

HEY, TOP-KNOT!
PAAA
HMM ?

I SUGGEST YOU DEFEND THIS PHENOM LIKE YOUR LIFE DEPENDED ON IT.

IF YOU WANT ANY CHANCE TO WIN.

SPIN

BUT EITHER WAY, YOUR FATE IS SEALED.

HA HA HA

QVR

SHK

TCH

...

...

RAAAAGH

WHAT'D YOU SAY?! I'LL KILL YOU, RED HEAD!!

HEY!!

WAAAAHAHA!!
YEAAH
HANA-MICHI'S ADDING FUEL TO THE FIRE ALREADY!
CLAP CLAP
CLAP CLAP
GO!
WHY ARE THEY BEING SO MEAN TO HIM?

DO THEY KNOW THIS IS JUST A BASKETBALL GAME?!
HEEEEY!
KILL 'EM!
I DUN-NO...
RAH

OKAY! IT'S JUST ABOUT TO START!
SKFF SKFF
WE MADE IT.

TOYO-TAMA!!

RAAA

HEY, NUMBER TEN!!

FOOL!!

DMM DMM

DON'T THINK YOU'RE GETTIN' OUTTA HERE ALIVE, REDHEAD!

AAAHHH

WHAT IS UP WITH ALL THIS NASTY HECKLING?
AH

...
HEY-!
THIS IS TICKING ME OFF!
IRK
GRR
GRR
LOSER!!
SCRUB-!!

DON'T LIS-TEN TO 'EM!
GO, HANA-MICHI!!

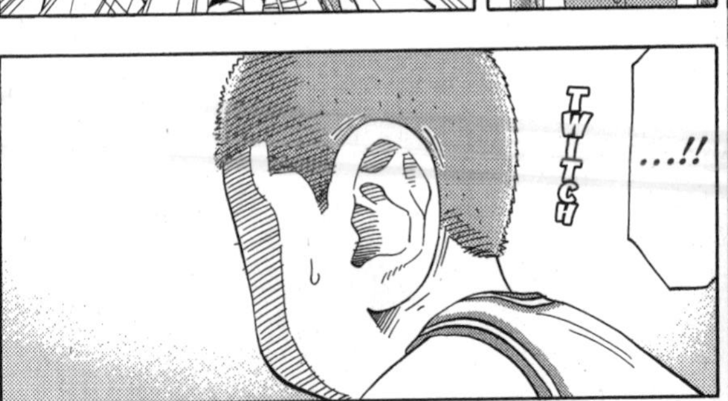
...!!
TWITCH

H-HARUKO ...?!
SHE CAME!

GOOOO!!
RAH

ALL THE WAY TO HIROSHIMA ... ♡
AWWWW
SHUR SHK

HEY! WE CAME TO SEE YOU, YOU RED-HEADED MONKEY!
GOINK
...

'CUZ IF WE DON'T WATCH THIS GAME, WE MAY NEVER SEE SHOHOKU AGAIN.
SNICKER...

YEAH
I DOUBT IT'LL BE THE KIND OF GAME EVERYBODY EXPECTS WHEN AN A-RANK TEAM PLAYS A C-RANK TEAM.
RAH
RAH
IT'S ABOUT TO START!
WOO

...

MOVE FAST.
YOU GOT IT.

(4) Takenori Akagi
Senior, 197 cm
(8) Mitsuaki Iwata
Senior, 190 cm
C
(Center)
PF
(Power Forward)
(10) Hanamichi Sakuragi
Freshman, 189 cm
WMP
BMP
(5) Minori Kishimoto
Freshman, 189 cm
(4) Tsuyoshi Minami
Senior, 184 cm
(11) Kaede Rukawa
Freshman, 187 cm
...
SF
(Small Forward)
(7) Kyohei Yajima
Senior, 180 cm
SG
(Shooting Guard)
(14) Hisashi Mitsui
Senior, 184 cm
(6) Daijiro Itakura
Junior, 183 cm
HUH? YOU'RE A STARTER?
(7) Ryota Miyagi
Junior, 168 cm
NO WAY!
PG
(Point Guard)
RAAAAH!!

HUP
SWP
HNGH!!

DASH
!!
SWAP
YES!!
IT'S THE SAME THING THEY DID AGAINST US!
GLARE
MMM...
PAA

?!
!!
PA
PAA
MIYAGI! PASS IT! WHAT'RE YOU DOING?!
NO!!
FW
HOW D'YOU LIKE THAT?
Funny face!

SWAP

!!

GASP!!

YEAH!!
WOOOO
DON'T TRY TO SHOW OFF, TWERP!

GULP!!

ALL RIGHT! GO!!
RAAAH
FAST BREAK!!

MINAMI!!
FWP

ROOOOAR

SHF

I GOT IT!

...

SWIP

!

H
OH YEAH!
UP
!!
SWSH
...
AHH!!
YES!!
DMM DMM DMM
BOOM!!
努力

READ THIS WAY

...

YOU ...!

CRAP!!

TMP

TMP

TMP

SHOHOKU'S GOING FOR A RUNNING GAME ALREADY!

THEY WANNA START TRADING BASKETS?!

...

!!

PAA

HE'S FAST!!

HE CUT INSIDE!
H
YA
GLARE
YOU LOOK LIKE YOU'RE SHOOT-ING...

SM
...BUT I KNOW YOU WANNA PASS!
!!
AP
A RANK, HUH...
!!

AA 山王工業
C 湘 北
A 豊 玉
B 熊本第

Chart: AA Sannoh Kogyo (Akita)
C Shohoku (Kanagawa)
A Toyotama (Osaka)
B Kumamoto Dai San

SLAM DUNK

SK
P
A
A
A-RANK ...
MINAMI !!

ANGRY PHENOM

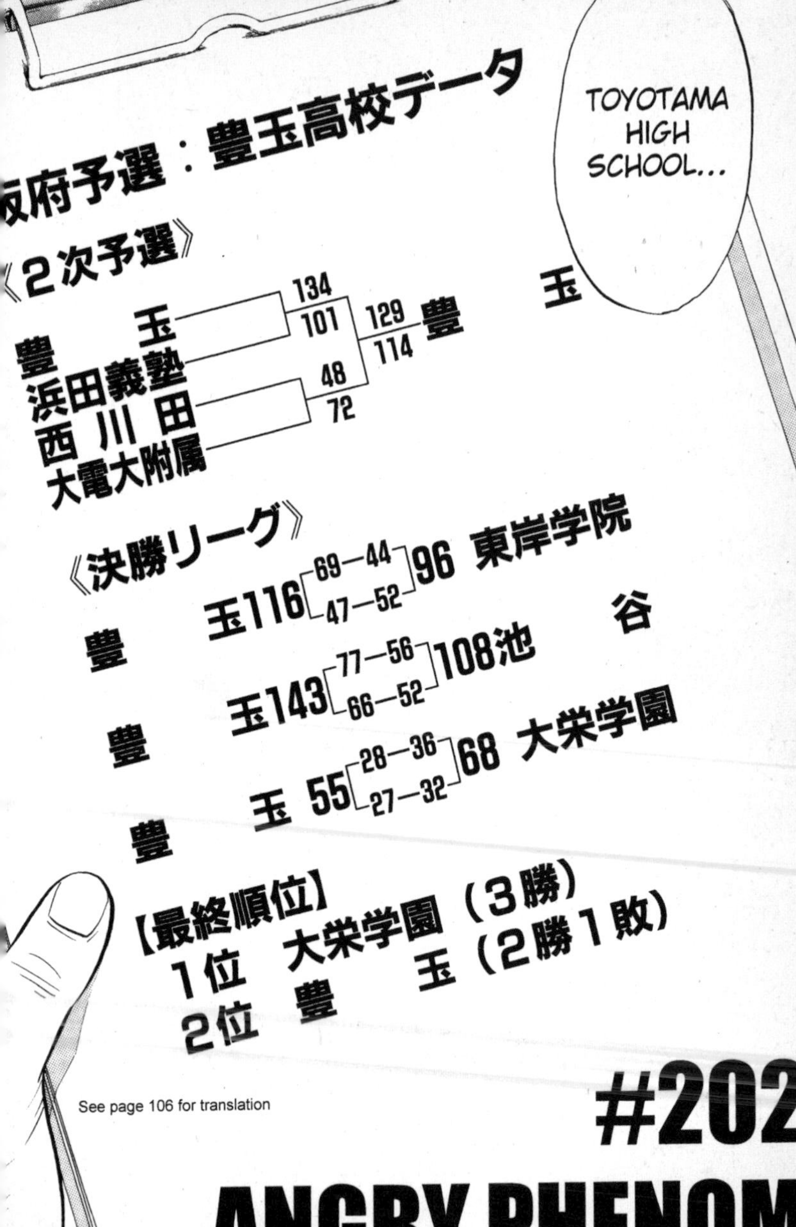
TOYOTAMA HIGH SCHOOL...
阪府予選：豊玉高校データ
《2次予選》
豊玉
浜田義塾
西川田
大電大附属
134
101
48
72
129
114
豊玉
《決勝リーグ》
豊玉116［69—44 47—52］96 東岸学院
豊玉143［77—56 66—52］108池谷
豊玉 55［28—36 27—32］68 大栄学園
【最終順位】
1位 大栄学園（3勝）
2位 豊玉（2勝1敗）

See page 106 for translation

#202 ANGRY PHENOM

THIS IS TOO EASY!!
PAAA
WHA—?!
YEAH!!
ROOAR
DMM DMM DMM
NICE ONE, KISHIMOTO!!

WHAM
HEY!!
AGH!

BUMP
!!
...

WHAAA?!

FWEEE—T

BONK
FOOL!!

AWWW
AW! HE GOT A FOUL!
CALM DOWN, SAKU-RAGI!
That was too obvious!
JUST DON'T GET CAUGHT, HANA-MICHI!!

GRR! HE BUMPED INTO ME FIRST!

OW! GEEZ! DOESN'T HE KNOW HIS OWN STRENGTH ...?!

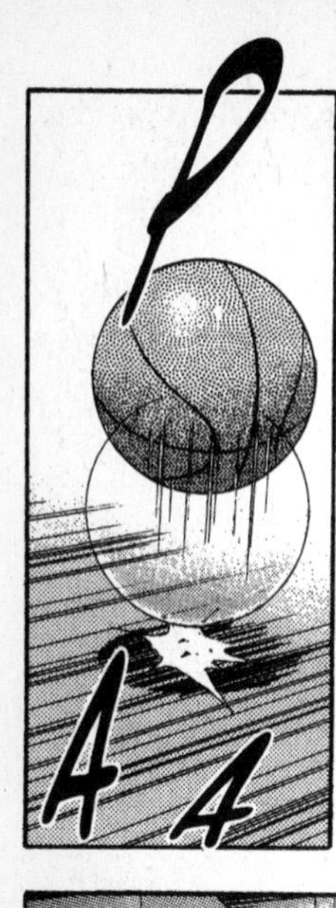

GA

NK

OW!!

PA

A

A

WOOOO!!

THAT WASN'T A FOUL?!

YO! YAJI !!

YEAH
OOOO!!
NICE, YAJIMA !!

NO! NO! NO!

NOT EVEN A MINUTE INTO THE GAME AND IT'S ALREADY SIX TO NOTHING!
WOH
豊玉
(大阪)
19:11
RAH
湘北
(神奈川)
SEIKO
6
0
YAY
YAH
NOT GOOD!!

Scoreboard: Shohoku Toyotama

AND AFTER ABOUT A MINUTE...
OVER HERE, ITA-KURA!
GIVE IT TO ME!
TOYOTA
5

THIS NUMBER 10 GUY IS A JOKE! PASS IT TO ME!
!!

READ THIS WAY

SMAP
GRR
YOU'RE DEAD!!

SWAP

FOOL.
!!
FWIP

FWP
TOYOTAMA
4

MINAMI
...

HE'S GOT A QUICK RELEASE!

SW
SH
YEAH! A THREE!!
WOOOOOOOO
DOMM DOMM DOMM
WE GOT THIS IN THE BAG!!
MI-NA-MI!!
湘北
(神奈川)
18:56
豊玉
(大阪)
SEIKO
1ST
MI-NA-MI!!
MI-NA-MI!!
UGH...

READ THIS WAY

GRRR...

GRIT

FUME

FRET

ARGH! WHY DO YOU GUYS ALWAYS START SO SLOW!

THEY'RE SCORING AT WILL!

DON'T LET THEM SCORE NINE IN ONE MINUTE!

THIS FAST PACE...
...IS TOYO-TAMA BASKET-BALL.
COACH.
What's with that shirt?
THEY'RE ALL SKILLED INDIVIDUALS, AS I SUSPECTED...

GEE, I WAS HOPING THEY'D AT LEAST WIN IN THE FIRST ROUND BUT...
HMPH
HMM
WE COULD BE HEADING HOME TODAY, THE WAY THINGS ARE GOING.
WHA
THAT'S VERY POSSIBLE.
Seriously.

THEY'RE REPRESENTING OSAKA— A VERY TIGHTLY CONTESTED REGION...
THEY'RE ALL GOOD...

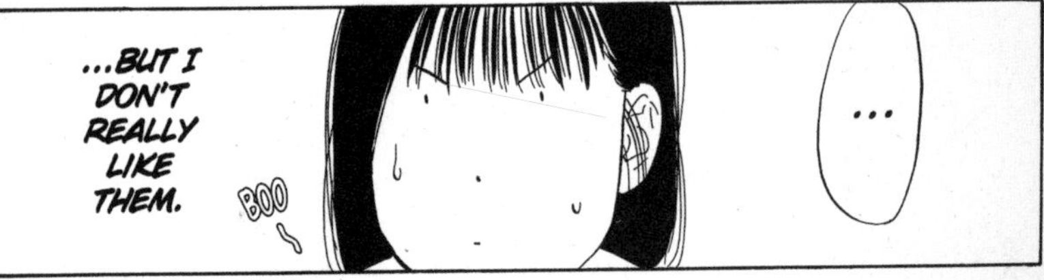
...
...BUT I DON'T REALLY LIKE THEM.
BOO

ROAAR

YOU'RE THE ACE, AREN'T YOU? NAGAREKAWA?

...

BE MORE AGGRESSIVE.

EXCEPT FOR THE DAIEI GAME THAT THEY LOST, THEY AVERAGED 130.5 POINTS IN THE OSAKA REGIONALS.
THEY EMPHASIZE OFFENSE.
TRADING BASKETS.
A RUNNING GAME.
WOO
WAH
YEAH
YAH

TOYATAMA HAS BEEN TO THE NATIONALS BEFORE, AND THEIR TRADITION REMAINS INTACT.
THEY MAY HAVE A NEW COACH, BUT THEIR STYLE HASN'T CHANGED AT ALL.

SO IT'S TOYOTAMA'S PACE SO FAR.
IT APPEARS SO.

...

BUT THEN AGAIN, SHOHOKU IS THE SAME TYPE OF TEAM...
WHAT DO YOU THINK, MAKI?

SHOYO LOST TO TOYOTAMA IN LAST YEAR'S NATIONALS DIDN'T THEY?

SHOYO ...?!

...

MOST LIKELY ...

THAT'S RIGHT, THEY DID.
THAT MEANS SHOHOKU IS IN FOR A TOUGH GAME.

IT COULD GET INTERESTING IF SAKURAGI'S IMPROVED SINCE THE REGIONALS...

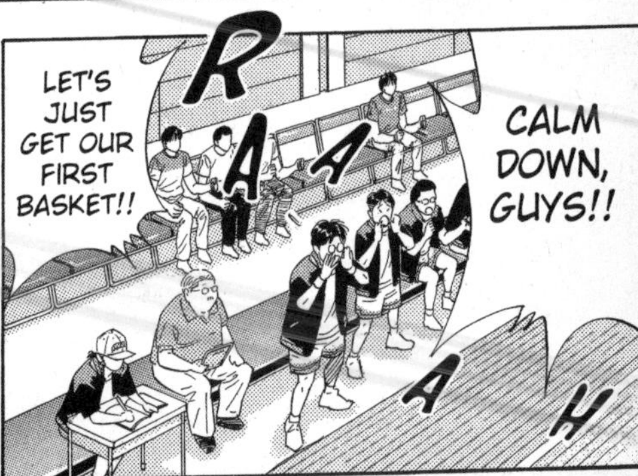
CALM DOWN, GUYS!!
LET'S JUST GET OUR FIRST BASKET!!
RAAAAH

RYOTA! DON'T FALL FOR THEIR TAUNTS!
PLAY YOUR REGULAR GAME!

READ THIS WAY

YOUR REGULAR GAME? HMM...
S'KWEE
WHAT'S THE MATTER? SHOW ME WHAT YOU GOT.

GRIN

...
FOOM

HEY, RED-HEAD!
RAH
DON'T TOUCH ME.

IS THERE ANY POINT IN ME EVEN DEFENDING YOU?
NRRH?

YOU HAVEN'T TOUCHED THE BALL ONCE YET.
ARE YOU ONE OF THOSE GUYS THEY NEVER PASS THE BALL TO?
GRR
...!!

WHOOSH

HEY!! RYOTA!! PASS!!

!!
HUH?

!!
YIPES

OH, HE'S MAD NOW!

YOU'RE GONNA BE SORRY, TOP-KNOT!!
SW
A
P

SORRY YOU MADE THIS PHENOM MAD!!

READ THIS WAY
IS HE GONNA DO IT?!
DO WHAT?
YES! HE HAS SPACE!
HE'S GONNA SHOOT FROM THERE?!

EAT THIS!! TRAINING CAMP SHOT!!

HMFF!!
SH
HWP
!!

GO!!
RULE THE
20
WHAT?

PAPP

HUH?!
SHOHOKU
10

HE'S LIKE HE USED TO BE!
WHUH
LIKE THE START OF TRAINING CAMP!
RULE
WORLD

...
TCH
TCH
TCH

IT'S SO SAD...
I CAN'T BELIEVE WE STRUG-GLED AGAINST THEM!

WAA
WHAT WAS THAT?!
HA HA HA HA
BWA HA HA HA HA!!
HA
NICE ONE, NUMBER 10!
HA

AND HE WAS SUBBED OUT.
DOOOM
NO WAY!

I GUESS IT WON'T BE THAT EASY...

TH-THAT WASN'T IT!
HA HA HA HA
C-CRAP!!
MORON.
HA! WASN'T WHAT?
SHOHOKU

I'M BETTER THAN THAT!
Damn!
ARGH
THAT WASN'T IT!

Osaka Regionals: Toyotama High School Data

<2nd Round>

Toyotama
Hamada Gijuku
Nishikawada
Daidendai Fuzoku

Toyotama

<Group League>

Toyotama	Togan Gakuin
Toyotama	Iketani
Toyotama	Daiei Gakuen

[Final Standings]
1st Daiei Gakuen (3 Wins)
2nd Toyotama (2 Wins 1 Loss)

大阪府予選：豊玉高校データ

《2次予選》

豊　玉 134	129	豊　玉
浜田義塾 101		
西川田 48	114	
大電大附属 72		

《決勝リーグ》

豊　玉 116	69—44 / 47—52	96	東岸学院
豊　玉 143	77—56 / 66—52	108	池　谷
豊　玉 55	28—36 / 27—32	68	大栄学園

【最終順位】
1位　大栄学園（3勝）
2位　豊　玉（2勝1敗）

That wasn't it...
SLAM DUNK

Scoreboard: Shohoku Toyotama

GORI ON A ROLL

湘北
(神奈川)
18:44
豊玉
(大阪)
0
SEIKO
1ST
9

NO WONDER THEY'RE REGULARS IN THE NATIONALS... THEY'RE ALL SO SKILLED!

TOYOTAMA—

RAH

WOO

RAH

YAH

YASUDA.

YES, COACH!

YAY

TOYOTAMA PLAYS A FAST-PACED HIGH SCORING GAME.

YEAH

WOH

IT'S DANGEROUS FOR US TO PLAY AT THEIR PACE.

SLOW THE PACE DOWN ...?
全国高

MIYAGI'S GOT TUNNEL VISION RIGHT NOW.
HE'S SUCH A HOTHEAD! SO UNDISCIPLINED!
YOU'RE GOING TO SLOW EVERYBODY DOWN. OKAY?
YES, SIR!

RAAH
ROAR
SHOHOKU
10
6
TOYOTAMA
6
#203
GORI ON A ROLL

READ THIS WAY

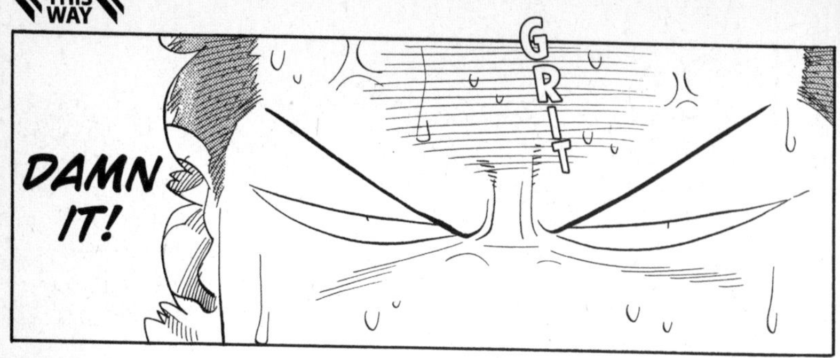
GRIT
DAMN IT!

HMPH! SO THEY ONLY USE HIM 'CUZ HE'S BIG.
SCRUB.

DON'T WORRY, SAKURAGI!
PLAY YOUR GAME!
GRR
!!
THAT SHOT WAS IN MY GAME!
BONK
!!

WHY'D YOU SUB ME, COACH?! YOU KNOW HOW GOOD I AM!!
WHACK
PAT PAT PAT
STOP THAT!
Not at the Nationals!
SAKURAGI, SUBBING ISN'T A PUNISHMENT.
WE NEED YASUDA SO WE CAN CHANGE THE PACE.
GRRRR
GRRRRR
SO THIS PHENOM IS INFERIOR TO YASUDA?!
WHUH~?
SIGH~...

WHY IS IT YASUDA AND NOT KOGURE?
BECAUSE IT'S A GUARD'S JOB.

UH-HUH. AND...

...HE MAY NOT LOOK IT, BUT YASUDA'S GOT REAL GUTS.
PLEASE LEAVE.
PLEASE.

...!!

HE WON'T LET THE TAUNTS AND HECKLING GET TO HIM.
WOO
YAH
大会
Are you sure?

DONK

HMFFF!!

バスケットボール

SWAP

!!

READ THIS WAY

SMAP

YES!!

NICE RE-BOUND!!

PA

LET'S GO!!

TMP

HEY! GONNA START PLAYING YOUR REGULAR GAME?

GRR

SHUT UP!!

TMP

RYOTA! STOP!!

HMM ?
GLARE

RYOTA! PASS!

I SEE... THEY CERTAINLY HAVE WON WITH INCREDIBLE SCORES...
134...129
116...
143...
THEIR GAME AGAINST DAIEI GAKUEN WAS THE ONLY LOW SCORING GAME, AND THEY LOST THAT.

GEEZ. YOU WASTED A CHANCE FOR A FAST BREAK.

GRIN

PAAA

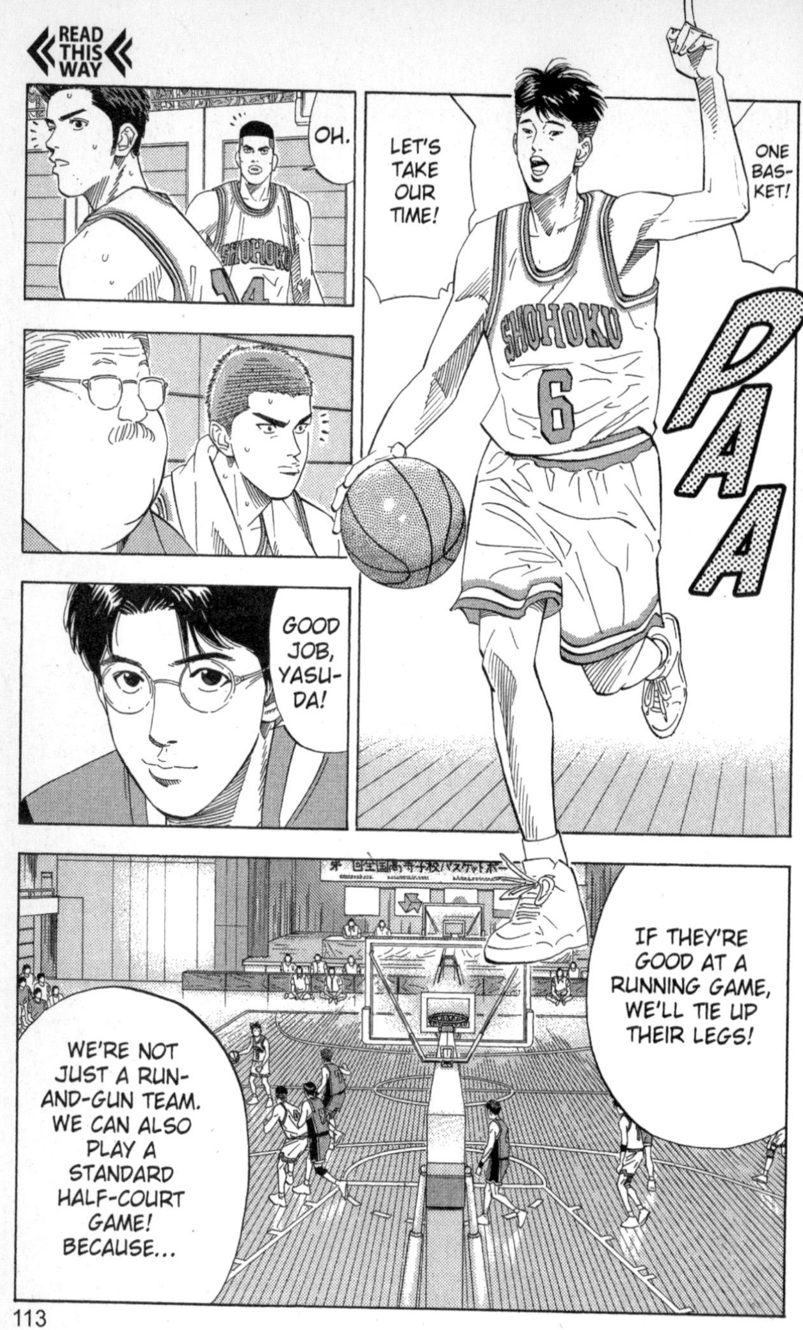
READ THIS WAY
ONE BAS-KET!
LET'S TAKE OUR TIME!
PAAA
OH.
GOOD JOB, YASU-DA!
IF THEY'RE GOOD AT A RUNNING GAME, WE'LL TIE UP THEIR LEGS!
WE'RE NOT JUST A RUN-AND-GUN TEAM. WE CAN ALSO PLAY A STANDARD HALF-COURT GAME! BECAUSE...

...WE HAVE KANA-GAWA'S KING OF THE INTERIOR, AKAGI!
TAKE YOUR TIME ON OFFENSE.
FEED THE BALL TO AKAGI AND BUILD THE GAME FROM DOWN LOW.
AKAGI!!
FWIP
SWAP

PAA
HUH?!
RAAAGH!!
LEAP
SH
FF

RAAAH
OH YEAH! YESS !!
AKAGI!!

...

...
YES!!

YEEEEAH!
GORI!
YES! YOUR FIRST POINTS AT THE NATION-ALS!

WOO!
I SEE. SO THAT'S THE PLAN.
GRIN
YAH!

WOW.
WHEN THEY GET POSSESSION, MOVE BACK QUICK...
...BEFORE THEY TRY TO PUSH IT UP COURT.

TMP
GET BACK! GET...

RAH!
TCH.

WAH!
WE WOULDN'T HAVE LOST TRADING BASKETS!

READ THIS WAY

WHAT TOOK YOU SO LONG, YASU?
WHOA !!
Sorry...
NO SENSE LETTING THEM GET A FAST BREAK.
SHOHOKU

MMPH!!

THEY GOT BACK ON DE-FENSE FAST!

SO THEY JUDGED TOYOTAMA TO BE EQUALS OR BETTER, AND DECIDED TO CHANGE THEIR STYLE.
THEY SLOWED THE GAME DOWN.

...
THE GAMESMAN IN HIM MUST BE REALLY BUZZING, COACHING AT THE NATIONALS ...

COACH ANZAI IS MAKING HIS MOVE EARLY TODAY.

WHOA!!
SPAK

GAMESMAN
...

WHY'RE YOU LOOKING ALL COOL?
HUH?
Put me in.
JIGGLE WIGGLE

!!

GO-RI!
THERE IT IS! THE FLY SWAT-TER...
...THE NATION-ALS VER-SION!!
WOOOOT

READ
THIS
WAY

F-FLY SWATTER ...?!
MURMER
CHATTER
WHOA...
BUZZ
BUZZ
THAT WAS AN INSANE BLOCK!
WOW
WHA
HMM

HE'S SO INTIMI- DATING!
NONE OF THE CENTERS IN OSAKA HAVE GOT THAT MUCH PRESENCE!
HF
HF

BE PA- TIENT!!
4
4
LET'S TAKE OUR TIME!!

FEH...

CENTER!!
THEY'RE GONNA TRY TO FINISH WITH THEIR CENTER! STOP HIM!
DENY HIM THE PASS!

SHUT UP!! I KNOW !!

SKFF

FWIP
!!
...!!

DUNK
4
TOYOTAMA

OOOOWAAH!!
YEAH!!
AAH
THERE IT IS!!
GORILLA DUNK ...?!
DAMN!!
I'VE NEVER SEEN A DUNK LIKE THAT!

READ THIS WAY

YAAA

WOO HOO!!

AKAGI'S GORILLA DUNK!!

WUMP

AKAGI'S A NATIONALS-CALIBER PLAYER NOW.

ROAAR

ANZAI'S STRATEGY PAID OFF.

FROM A 9-0 SCORE AFTER THE FIRST MINUTE, IN THE FOLLOWING TEN MINUTES...

...THEY CLOSED THE GAP TO 15-14. AT THE TEN-MINUTE MARK, IT WAS CLEAR THIS WAS NOT GOING TO BE A 100-POINT GAME.

TH...
WHU H?
THEY CAUGHT UP AFTER I LEFT THE GAME.

...!!

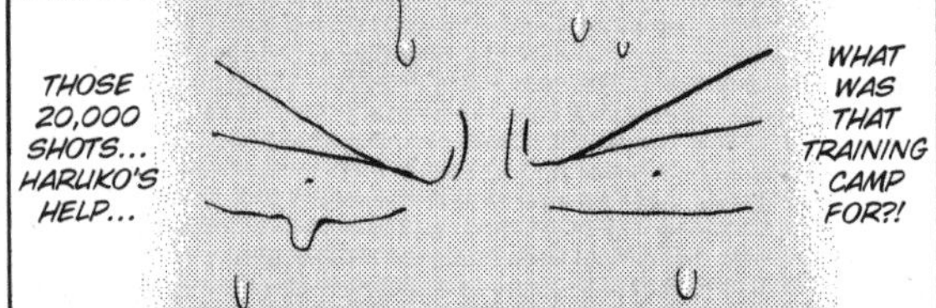
WHAT WAS THAT TRAINING CAMP FOR?!
THOSE 20,000 SHOTS... HARUKO'S HELP...

...
QUIVER
...

HEY, OLD MAN! I'M GOING BACK IN SOON, RIGHT? RIGHT? RIGHT?!
YAAARRGH
YOU KNOW MY SKILLS! YOU TAUGHT 'EM TO ME!
PAT PAT PAT PAT
C-C-CALM DOWN, SAKU-RAGI!!
I'M GONNA GET TO PLAY, RIGHT?!

Y-YOU'VE GOT IT WRONG, SAKURAGI!
IT WAS JUST A STRATEGIC DECISION...
OLD MAN!!

OF COURSE YOU WILL.
HMPH
!!

AS OUR TRUMP CARD.

...

TRUMP CARD ...?

GRIN

WELL, AKAGI SEEMS TO BE ON A ROLL TODAY. WE COULD BE TAKING THE LEAD.

Hey, wait a minute. If we take the lead here, we might not need a trump card!
You're not trying to trick me again, are you ...?
GULP

SLAM DUNK

CHAT
BUZZ
WHO IS THAT GUY?!
THAT NUMBER FOUR?
BUZZ
WAH
CHAT
WHAT'S THAT BUFF CENTER'S NAME?

AKAGI, HUH?
MUMBL
BUZZ
I NEVER HEARD OF HIM.

WOH
I NEVER HEARD OF SHOHOKU, ACTUALLY.
THEY GOOD?
CHAT

THEY'RE HOLDING THEIR OWN AGAINST TOYOTAMA! THAT MEANS THEY'RE GOOD!
BUZZ
WHA
湘北 (神奈川) 9:29 豊玉 (大阪)
SEIKO
14 1ST 17

THERE HE GOES AGAIN!!

Scoreboard: Shohoku Toyotama

#204
JUMP SHOT
UNGH!!
IT'S AKAGI!!
SHOHOKU

READ THIS WAY

OOOWAH!!

SMACK

YEAH!!

TSK
CRAP!!
HF
HF

YOU SEE THAT, TOYO-TAMA !!
THAT'S KANA-GAWA'S NUMBER ONE CENTER, AKAGI!

UOZUMI ...

AKAGI, I ALWAYS KNEW...
...THAT YOU WERE A NATIONAL-LEVEL PLAYER.

YOU WERE WAY BETTER !!

RAH
SANNOH
SANNOH
WOO
YAH
HE'S A GOOD CENTER ...
WHOA! IS THAT SANNOH ?!
THAT'S SANNOH KOGYO!
Sannoh Kogyo Coach
Goro Domoto

WOH
WAH
YAY

I WONDER WHAT THE CHAMPS THINK OF SHOHOKU ...?

IWATA! WHAT'RE YOU DOING TRYING TO PLAY HIM STRAIGHT UP?!
THAT CENTER'S WAY BETTER THAN YOU! YOU SHOULD KNOW BETTER THAN TO PLAY HIM LIKE THAT!

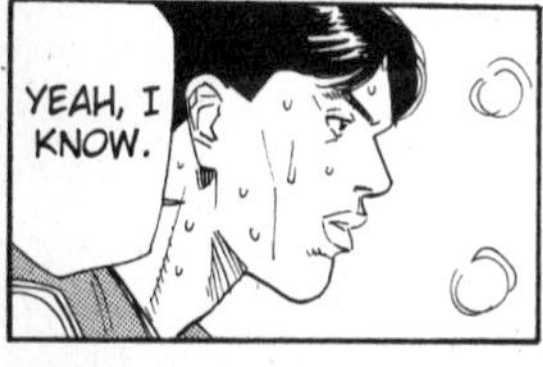
YEAH, I KNOW.

...
GLARE

C'MON! LET'S GET ONE!
PAA
WOH!
HEY!!
YEAH!
RAAAA
WHAT'RE YOU DOIN' SLOWING THE GAME DOWN, TWERP?!
I'LL KILL YOU!!
WHAT'RE YOU TRYING TO DO?!
努力
豊玉高等学校バスケット部

Banner: *Doryoku* (effort/hard work)
Toyotama High School Basketball Team

AAH
GULP

NOW, NOW. WAIT GUYS!
IT CAN'T BE HELPED!!

THEY HAVE TO PLAY IT SLOW!
BECAUSE THE ACE IS SITTIN' ON THE BENCH!

HEH HEH HEH
THE TRUMP CARD!
ZWA—AH

ONCE THIS ACE STEPS IN, WE'LL BE MORE AGGRESSIVE, SO SHUT YOUR MOUTHS!

ROAAR
What'd you say?!
WHAT PART OF YOU IS THE ACE, FOOL!
MORON!

SHOHO-KU'S PLAN IS CLEAR.
THEY'RE TAKING THEIR TIME ON OFFENSE TO KEEP THIS A LOW SCORING GAME.
AND THEY'RE GONNA TRY TO SCORE WITH THEIR MOST RELIABLE THREAT, AKAGI!
WE GOTTA STOP AKAGI!

SHIFT

TRIPLE-TEAM!!

GOOD!!
FWIP
?!
BUMP

READ THIS WAY

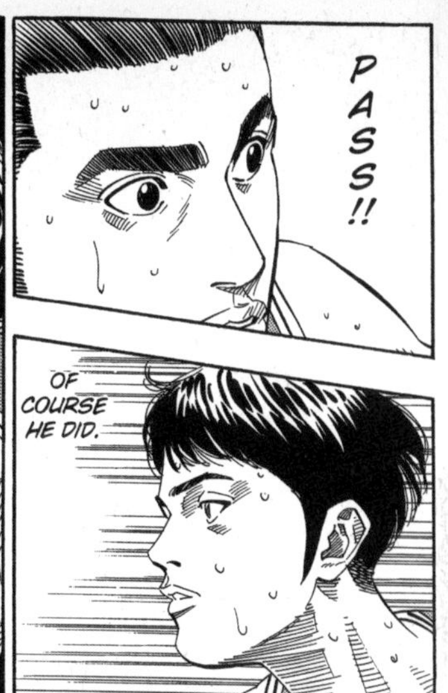
PASS!!
OF COURSE HE DID.

NAGARE-KAWA, IF YOU REALLY ARE THE ACE!

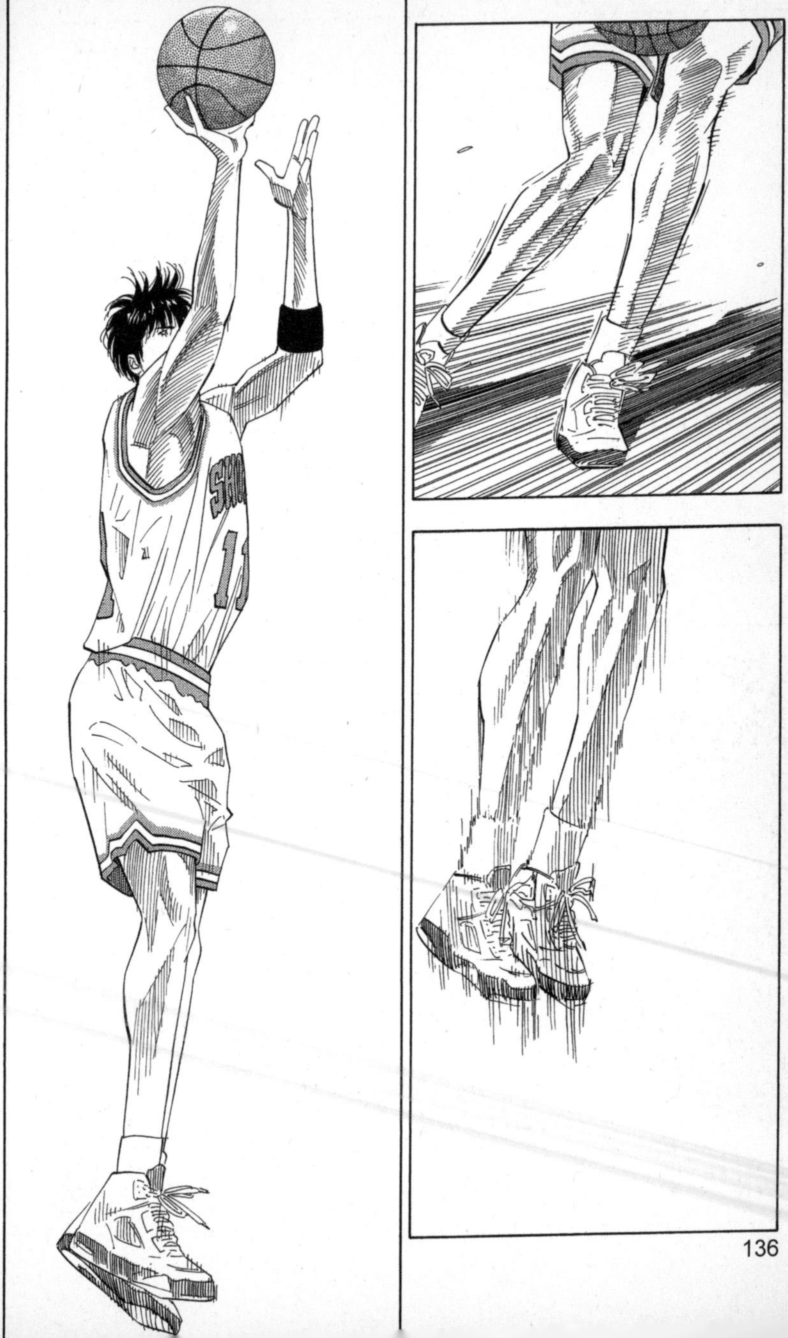

READ THIS WAY

!!

WHAT?!

THAT WAS FAST!

AND HE'S GOT A HIGH RELEASE POINT!

HE FINALLY REALIZED HOW INCREDIBLE IT WAS.

AFTER TAKING 20,000 JUMP SHOTS IN TRAINING CAMP, FOR THE FIRST TIME SAKURAGI REALIZED JUST HOW AMAZING RUKAWA'S SHOT WAS.

SWISH

WHOA! THEY'RE IN THE LEAD!
RAAAAH
YES!!
RU-KAWA ♡
RU-KAWA ♡
湘北 (神奈川)
8:51
豊玉 (大阪)
18
SEIKO
1ST
17
Scoreboard: Shohoku Toyotama
SHOHOKU 11
SAKURAGI HADN'T REALIZED, BUT...
...RUKAWA'S PERFECT SHOT WAS THE ONE HE KEPT ENVISIONING FOR HIMSELF WHILE MAKING THOSE 20,000 SHOTS.

WOH
AKAGI.
YEAH
HMM?
YAH
I'M FEELING IT TODAY, TOO.
SNAP
SNAP
OKAY.
I'LL DRAW THEM IN AND DISH IT OUT TO YOU.
HEH
TOYOTAMA QUICKLY REGAINED THE LEAD WITH MINAMI'S SECOND THREE-POINTER OF THE DAY.
SHOHOKU (Kangawa) 18
TOYOTAMA (Osaka) 20
1ST HALF 8:42
YEAH!! NICE, MINA-MI!!
WOOOO T
HE'S PLAYING FOR REAL NOW!
MINA-MI!!

READ THIS WAY

SHIFT
IT'S AKAGI! GET ON HIM!!
BUT MINAMI WAS ONLY PRE-TENDING.

HE HADN'T LEFT HIS ASSIGNMENT DEFENDING THE FRESHMAN PLAYER WHO HAD PUT UP ACE-CALIBER NUMBERS AT THE REGIONALS.

SWAP

SKWEE

WHOA! NICE D!

DAA

SHOHOKU
11

SHOHOKU
11
4

JUST FROM LOOKING AT HIS JUMP SHOT YOU CAN SEE HE'S GOT TALENT.
AND HIS ENTIRE BODY IS LIKE A SPRING!

!!

SWISH
YEAH!!
BEAUTIFUL!♡
YEEAAAH
WAY TO GO, RUKAWA!!
WOO
I THINK RUKAWA JUST GOT BETTER AGAIN!
HUH?! HE DID THAT AGAINST US, TOO.
HMPH
RAH
I DUNNO. I JUST GOT THAT FEELING.
YAH
BUZZ
THAT'S A REAL GOOD PLAYER.
I HEAR HE'S ONLY A FRESHMAN.
MURMUR
BUZZ
A FRESHMAN!
RUKAWA'S ALREADY MAKING A NAME FOR HIMSELF IN THE NATIONALS!
THE CROWD'S BUZZING!
CHAT
CHAT
YEAH.
HE MIGHT BECOME THE CENTER OF ATTENTION AT THIS TOURNAMENT!
GRR...
GRR...

READ THIS WAY

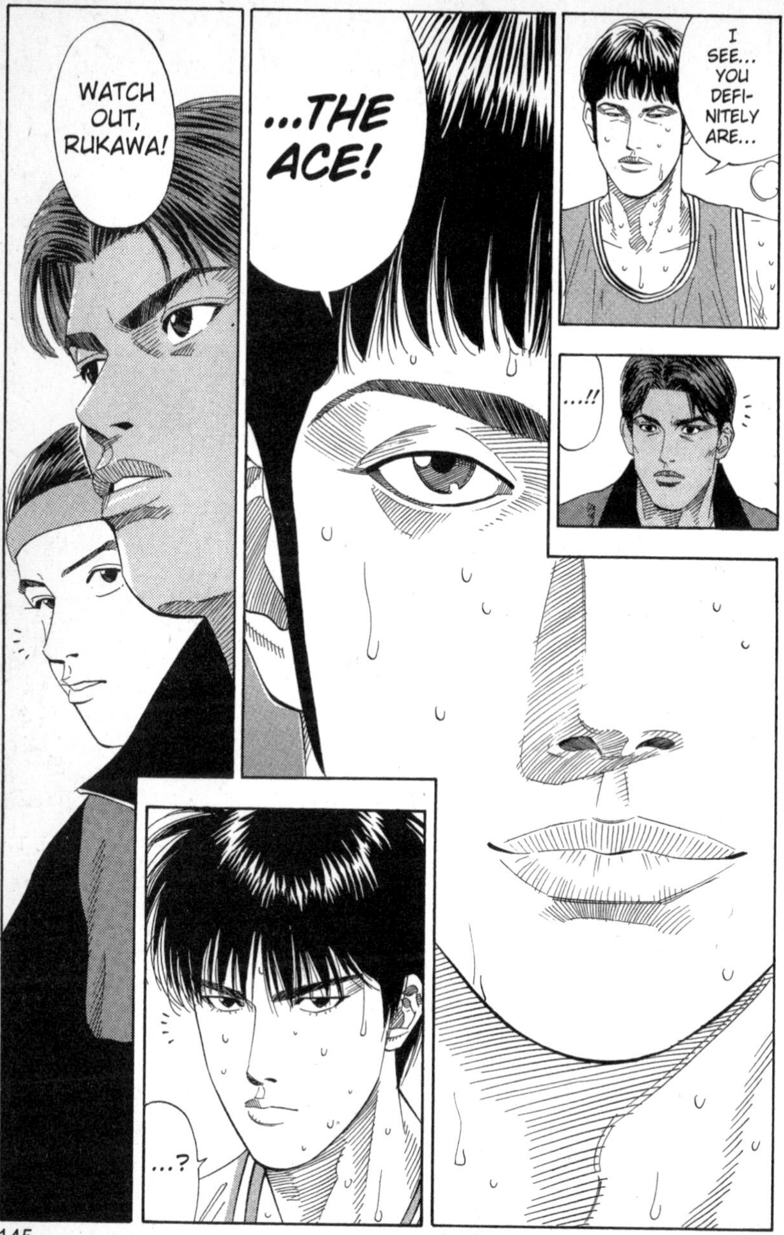

I SEE... YOU DEFINITELY ARE...

...THE ACE!

...!!

WATCH OUT, RUKAWA!

...?

You don't have to tell me. I already knew that!
Don't get cocky!!
SHOHOKU 11

SLAM DUNK

READ THIS WAY

WOO!
IT MIGHT LOOK LIKE RUKAWA'S SCORING AT WILL, BUT THAT'S NOT THE CASE.
NUMBER 4'S DEFENSE IS REALLY GOOD! YOU SAW HOW QUICK HIS FEET ARE.
RAH!

WOH!
YAH!
SO THAT MEANS OUR ACE IS BETTER THAN THEIRS!

WOW! I'M NERVOUS JUST SITTING HERE!

LOOKS LIKE THE CROWD'S ATTITUDE TOWARD US IS CHANGING A LITTLE.
BUZZ
BUZZ
MRMR

GOOD.
MUMBL
IT'S NO FLUKE THAT THEY CHAL-LENGED KAINAN.
CHAT
CHAT
THEY'RE TOUGH!
WOO
WOH
NUMBER 4 AND NUMBER 11...
BUZZ

THE ALLEGED ACE KILLER

#205
MRMR
NUMBERS 4 AND 11 ARE UNKNOWNS, BUT THEY'RE THE REAL DEAL!
BUZZ
CHAT
CHAT
BUZZ
WOH
MUMBL
THE ALLEGED ACE KILLER

READ THIS WAY

HMPH...
HAR-RUMPH...
AYAKO...
HMM?

WHEN DID RUKAWA...
...THAT SLY FOX, WHEN WAS HE PRACTICING?
...!

DEFENSE!!
LET'S STOP 'EM!!
YEAH!!
THEY'RE PLAYING LIKE THEY NORMALLY DO NOW!
THEY'RE GETTING INTO THE GAME!

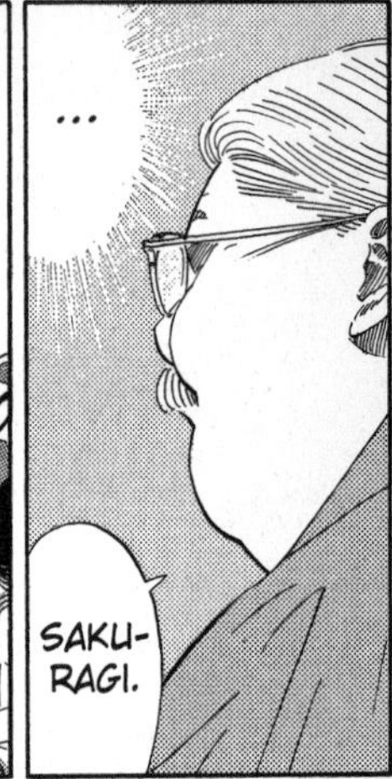
...
SAKU-RAGI.

DO YOU KNOW HOW MANY FAKES RUKAWA SHOWED BEFORE HE TOOK THE SHOT?
YEAH!
WOO!
HUH?

RAH!
HE FAKED RIGHT THEN LEFT...
WOH!

PAA
...THEN DROVE PAST HIM ON THE RIGHT.
SO, TWO FAKES.

THREE. HE HAS ANOTHER SUBTLE SHOT-FAKE AFTER THE LEFT ONE.

WHAT ?!

WATCH HIM CLOSELY.
STEAL EVERY-THING YOU CAN.

AND PRACTICE THREE TIMES AS MUCH AS HE DOES.
OTHER-WISE...

READ THIS WAY

...YOU'LL SPEND YOUR WHOLE HIGH SCHOOL CAREER PLAYING AND **NEVER** BE AS GOOD AS HE IS.
SHOHOKU 11
AMA 8
...!!

HE WAS ALREADY REALLY GOOD WHEN HE ENROLLED AT TOMIGAOKA JUNIOR HIGH.
THAT "FOX."
!!

RAH
SO IT'S OUR DIFFERENCE IN EXPERIENCE...
HUH.

WOO
OOOO!

WAIT! THAT MEANS YOU'RE SAYING THAT RIGHT NOW HE'S BETTER THAN ME!

YAH

I WON'T ADMIT THAT!

HE'S SO STUBBORN!

NO, NO, NO!!
I'll never admit it!

FROM THAT POINT ON, SAKURAGI BEGAN TO WATCH RUKAWA'S PLAY CLOSELY.
IT WOULD HELP HIM ACCELERATE HIS OWN GROWTH AS A PLAYER, BUT...

YEAH
...THAT'S A BIT FURTHER DOWN THE ROAD.
RAH
WHADDYA MEAN, "WATCH OUT, RUKAWA"?
IS SOMETHING WRONG, MAKI?

WOH
THAT NUMBER 4...
MINAMI.

READ THIS WAY

THE TEAM THEY WERE PLAYING, TOYO-TAMA, WAS NOT AN EASY OPPONENT.

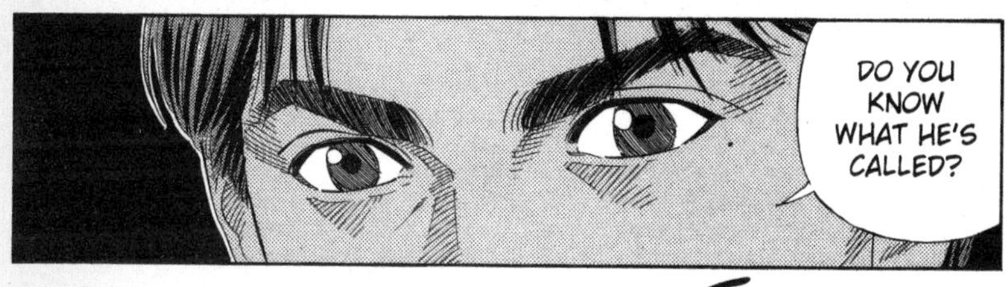
DO YOU KNOW WHAT HE'S CALLED?

SQUEAK
SQUEAK

YEAH! NICE, RUKAWA!!

RAAAH
NICE DEFENSE !!
BTING

READ
THIS
WAY

HEADS UP!!

WMMP

HUFF
HUFF
HUFF

MAN, HE'S SWEATING!
HOW MANY LAPS HAS THE BASKETBALL TEAM RUN?!

ISN'T TODAY ...
...THE START OF THE NATIONALS?
SHF
SKF
SHF
SKF
SHF
SKF

...

Thanks!

I HEAR SHOHOKU'S PLAYING TOYOTAMA.
SHF
HF
SKF
SHF
TOYO-TAMA ?!
SKF

SWWP
!!

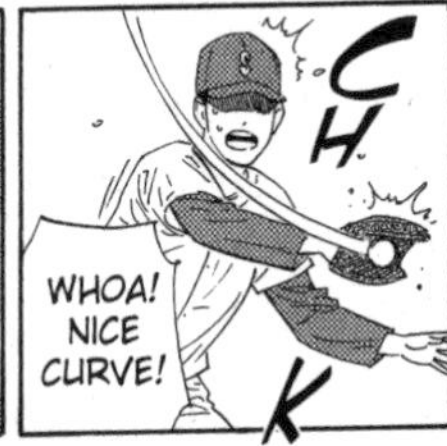
CH
K
WHOA! NICE CURVE!

SUMMER'S OVER.

FOR SHOYO— FOR US— THE WINTER INVITATIONAL IS EVERYTHING.
TOYO-TAMA'S NOT OUR CON-CERN.
HFF
HFF
HFF

READ THIS WAY

BUT SHOHOKU...
SHF
SKF
HF
HF
SHF
SKF

...BETTER NOT UNDER-ESTIMATE TOYOTAMA'S WILL TO WIN. ESPECIALLY...
SHF
SKF
SHF

SKF
...MINAMI'S!
SHF
SKF

SHF

ROOAAR
翔陽
(神奈川)
9:11
豊玉
(大阪)
33
SEIKO
1ST
36

Scoreboard: Shohoku Toyotama

SWSH
HE SCORED AGAIN!!
YEAH, FUJIMA!!
DANG, FUJIMA!
YEAAH
HE'S GOT TWENTY POINTS ALREADY!
YES!!
RAH
RAH

NOT BAD.
...!
SWAP
EVEN THOUGH YOU'RE THE ONLY JUNIOR IN THE STARTING LINEUP...
...YOU'RE CLEARLY THE ACE!
HM.

WHAM

RUKAWA!!

HWOOO

SKF
HFF
SHF
SKF
HFF

THEY CALL TSUYOSHI MINAMI...

... "THE ACE KILLER."

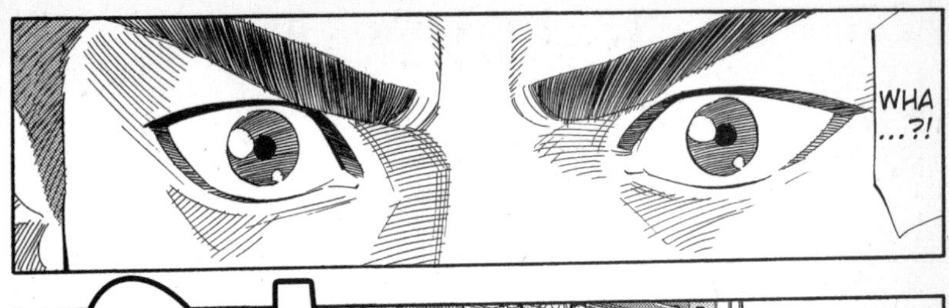
WHA ...?!

YOU DID THAT ON PURPOSE!!
SAKU-RAGI!!
DA
SH

?!
WHAT THE—?!
Why?

WHAT'D YOU SAY?!
STOP TALKING CRAP!

STOP, SAKU-RAGI!!
YANK
STOP THAT!
LET ME GO, GORI! THAT WAS INTENTION-AL!!

READ THIS WAY

SHUT UP! YOU CAN'T FOOL ME!
CALM DOWN OR I'LL EJECT YOU!

GET A STRETCHER!!
WOW
WOW
HE HAS A CONCUSSION!
OOH
UGH

HE GOT HIM GOOD!
IT WAS AN ELBOW.

YOU'RE GOING DOWN!

MINAMI... YESTERDAY YOU SAID WIN OR LOSE, NO HARD FEELINGS.
IS THIS WHAT YOU MEANT?

Hmm...
Article 71. When a player on the bench leaves the team bench area it's a technical foul. Oh... I see.
That's a technical on you.
WHAT?!
RULE
SLAM DUNK

WE ARE BEGINNERS

IT'S AKAGI!! STOP HIM!!

WHOA! THEY'RE REALLY CLAMPING DOWN ON AKAGI!

AAAGH!!

WHAM
!!
#206
WE ARE BEGINNERS
FWEET
HEEEEY!!

READ THIS WAY

FOUL! BLUE NUMBER EIGHT!
OOPS!

...

MPH
HMPH
NOOO! STOP, AKAGI!
AKAGI !!

THE GAME GOT VERY PHYSICAL.
BUZZ
BUZZ
WAH
WOH

MINAMI WAS ASSESSED AN INTENTIONAL FOUL FOR HIS ELBOW, BUT...

...THERE WAS NO WAY TO KNOW FOR SURE WHETHER IT WAS OR NOT.

WAY TO GO, TOYO-TAMA!
OOH!

EITHER WAY, SHOHOKU LOST THEIR LEAD SCORER.

HUH?!

WSSH
...
DON'T BE WUSSES!

THAT'S MORE LIKE TACKLING THAN DEFENSE!
DON'T HIDE!

GORI'S ABOUT TO LOSE IT, TOO.
THEY'RE ALL OVER HIM.

PA
PA
PA
A
IF THEY FOCUS ON AKAGI, THAT LEAVES THE REST OF US OPEN!
WH
YOU AIN'T OPEN!
MO- RON!
!!
AM

YEAH!!
FWEEET
KRASH
WHOA!!

RAH
WINK
SORRY! YOU OKAY, BUDDY?
WOH
OH!
NO, MIYAGI! DON'T!

RYOTA!!

READ THIS WAY

...!!
SKCH

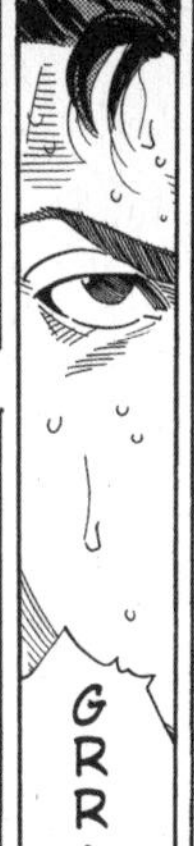
GRR...

BOTH CAP-TAINS!

IT'S OKAY TO GET PHYSICAL, BUT KEEP IT IN THE GAME!
YOU UNDER-STAND ?!

THIS IS YOUR ONLY WARNING.

HF
...
HF

THE END OF THE FIRST HALF.
ROAAR
BUZZ
BUZZ
MUMBL
MUTTR

HF
HF
...

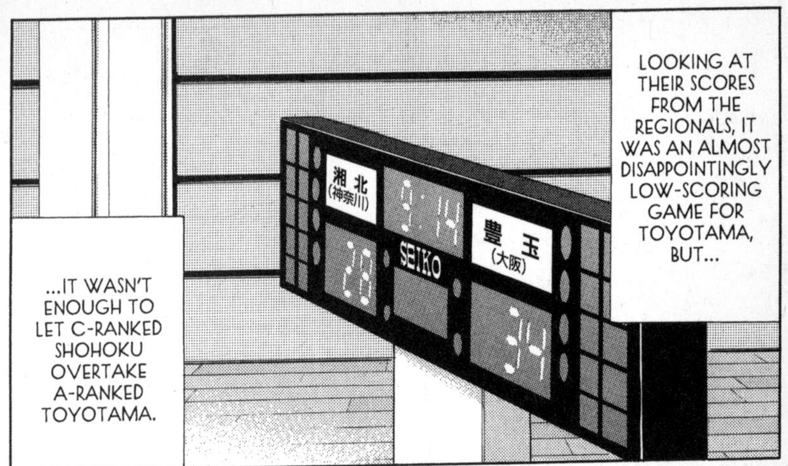
LOOKING AT THEIR SCORES FROM THE REGIONALS, IT WAS AN ALMOST DISAPPOINTINGLY LOW-SCORING GAME FOR TOYOTAMA, BUT...
...IT WASN'T ENOUGH TO LET C-RANKED SHOHOKU OVERTAKE A-RANKED TOYOTAMA.
湘北
(神奈川)
SEIKO
豊玉
(大阪)
28
34

Scoreboard: Shohoku Toyotama

LOOKS LIKE MINAMI'S ELBOW HAD AN AFFECT.
THAT WAS ON PUR-POSE!
THERE'S NO PROOF.
...!!
WHAT WILL YOU DO, SHOHOKU?

RRRAGH!!
THOSE JERKS !!
BONK
SQUEAK
HMPH.
DON'T BREAK IT.

READ THIS WAY

HOW'S RUKAWA?
HE'S IN THE INFIRMARY.

WHY WOULD I GO CHECK ON THAT FLIMSY FOX?
CHOKE
SKSH
GAH! BECAUSE WHEN HE WENT DOWN...
GRR
HUH?
NGH
...YOU JUMPED OFF THE BENCH...
...even though you got a technical for it!
I THOUGHT MAYBE YOU TWO WERE GETTING TO BE BUDDIES.
CHK

WSSH
I'LL GO CHECK.

HMM?

YOU WANNA COME TOO, SAKURAGI?

...
AAAAH
SQUASH
MISH
MASH
MUSH
P-PLEASE STOP!
SQUISH
WON'T HELP BECAUSE THEY'RE FRUSTRATED WITH TOYOTAMA'S ROUGH PLAY.
ALSO, THEY'RE TOO EXHAUSTED.

BONK
AGH!

LISTEN CAREFULLY, YOU FRESHMAN SQUIRT!!
LOOM

...
STAYING OUT OF IT.

IT'S BECAUSE ***I'M*** THE ONE WHO'S GONNA BEAT RUKAWA.

EVEN-TUALLY.

I WAS IN THE MIDST OF STUDYING HIS MANY WEAKNESSES WHEN THAT JERK INTERRUPTED ME!
PEEP
YOU GOT THAT, FRESH-MAN?!
YOU'RE A FRESH-MAN, TOO!
And a jerk!

NOW YOU KNOW!
IF WE PLAY GOOD DEFENSE, WE CAN WIN A LOW-SCORING GAME, TOO!
WE'VE GOT A FEW TOO MANY FOULS, THOUGH.

GOOD JOB! GOOD JOB! GOOD SCORE!
WATCH THAT IN THE SECOND-HALF!
SHUT UP.
HEY...
...!!

READ THIS WAY

WE'RE GONNA SCORE SIXTY POINTS IN THE SECOND-HALF.

WE'RE GOING ON A RUN.

H- HOLD ON, MINAMI!

WE PLAYED A GOOD FIRST HALF! THERE'S NO NEED TO UP THE PACE!

THAT WAS SHOHOKU'S PACE.

WE GOT CAUGHT IN THEIR SLOW PACE.

THAT'S WHY THE FOULS PILED UP.

...

IF THEY WANNA KEEP PLAYING SLOW, WE'LL GO FULL-COURT※ ON THEM.
MINA-MI!
LOOK FOR CHANCES TO STEAL THE BALL.
IF THEY BEAT US, SO BE IT.
THIS IS THE NATIONALS! IF WE LOSE IT'S OVER!
WE'RE GONNA WIN!

TOYOTAMA PLAYS A RUN-AND-GUN GAME!

※ Full-court (Full-court press)—Applying defensive pressure in the entire length of the court.

WE'RE GONNA WIN PLAYING RUN-AND-GUN!

...

HUH?!
GET REAL!
!!

FOR YEARS YOU'VE STALLED AT THE FINAL EIGHT WITH THAT RUN-AND-GUN STYLE.
COACH KITANO PROVED YOU CAN'T WIN A CHAMPIONSHIP LIKE THAT!
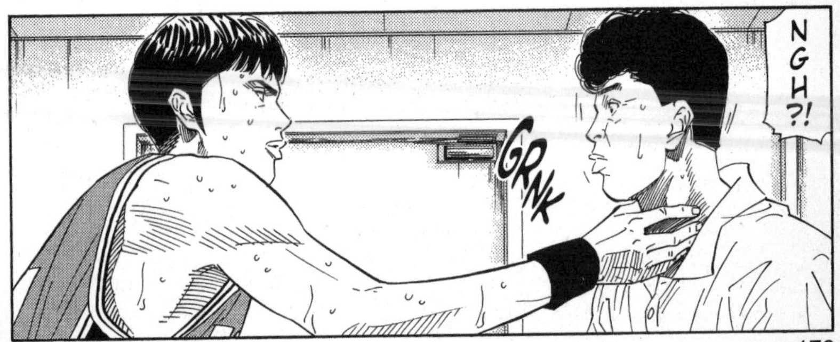
NGH?!
GRNK

READ THIS WAY

YOU WANNA DIE?

STOP, MINAMI!
THAT'S TOO MUCH!
MINAMI!!
HACK. COUGH.
WHAT ARE YOU THINKING, MINAMI?
COUGH.
ARE YOU OUT THERE WATCHING US, COACH KITANO?
...
WHAT'RE YOU PUNKS DOING HERE?!
ONLY AUTHORIZED PERSONNEL ALLOWED ON THE FLOOR.

HEH HEH.
C'MON! PLEASE?

TOYO-TAMA'S SO COOL.
THEY SCORE A HUNDRED POINTS EVERY GAME!
RUN-AND-GUN!
IT'S AWE-SOME!
WE WANNA SEE THEM UP CLOSE.
YEAAH

IS THAT SO ...?

HEY, BOYS! GO BACK UPSTAIRS.
YIPES
IT'S ALL RIGHT.

THESE ARE MY GRANDKIDS, UHHH... ICHIRO AND JIRO.

R-RIGHT!

READ THIS WAY

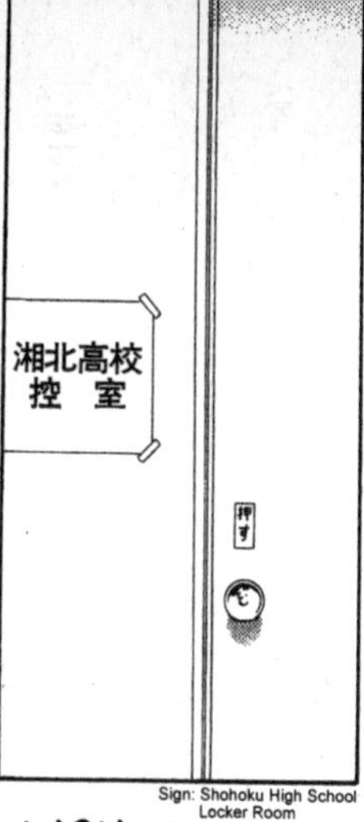
湘北高校
控室
押す
Sign: Shohoku High School Locker Room

...
?

HUSH
COACH HASN'T SAID A WORD YET!
IS HE ANGRY ...?

COACH, IT'S ALMOST TIME.

ANY INSTRUCTIONS FOR THE SECOND HALF?

WHY SO QUIET, OLD MAN? YOU HUNGRY OR SOMETHING?
TUG
S-STOP!

...

OUR POINT GUARD FALLS FOR THE OPPONENT'S CHEAP TAUNTS AND PLAYS SELFISHLY.
GULP
...!!

...

OUR CAPTAIN TRIES TO BULL HIS WAY THROUGH A TIGHT DEFENSE THAT WAS EXPECTING IT.
BDMP
...!!

WAS ALL THAT TALK ABOUT WINNING A NATIONAL TITLE...
...REALLY JUST TALK?

THAT'S WHY I ASKED, OLD MAN.
TUG
STETCH
PUT ME IN! I'LL PLAY HARD!
HANA-MICHI SAKU-RAGI!!
Cut that out!

CREAK

...!!

GASP!!

RUKA-WA!!
Ugh!

OOOH! THAT LOOKS LIKE IT HURTS! WHOA!
YIKES
YOU TOUCH IT AND YOU DIE.

RUKA-WA!
YOU GONNA PLAY IN THE SECOND HALF?!
OF COURSE.

HAS HE GOT ANY DEPTH PERCEP-TION?
THAT'S CRAZY!

LET'S DO THAT THING...

...THAT "WE ARE" THING.

...!!

READ
THIS
WAY

COACH IS RIGHT. I LOST MY HEAD OUT THERE... I'M STILL A BEGINNER.
MY BAD.
WE'RE GONNA HAVE TO LAY IT ALL ON THE LINE IN THE SECOND HALF!
PLAY ME!
ALL RIGHT. IT ALL COMES DOWN TO THE SECOND HALF.
LET'S DO IT.
...

WE. ARE. SHO-HO-KU!!

ALL RIGHT! NOW, HERE'S OUR STRATEGY FOR THE SECOND HALF.
GRIN

TO BE CONTINUED!

Coming Next Volume

It's the second half of Shohoku's debut game in the National Championship. Toyotama boasts the top three scorers from the Osaka regionals, and they're bent on nothing less than crushing Shohoku! But Coach Anzai's got a plan: steal the ball, run and score, facing Toyotama's run-and-gun style head-on! If Shohoku can't beat Toyotama at their best game, what chance do they have of beating last year's champion Sannoh in the next round?

ON SALE OCTOBER 2012

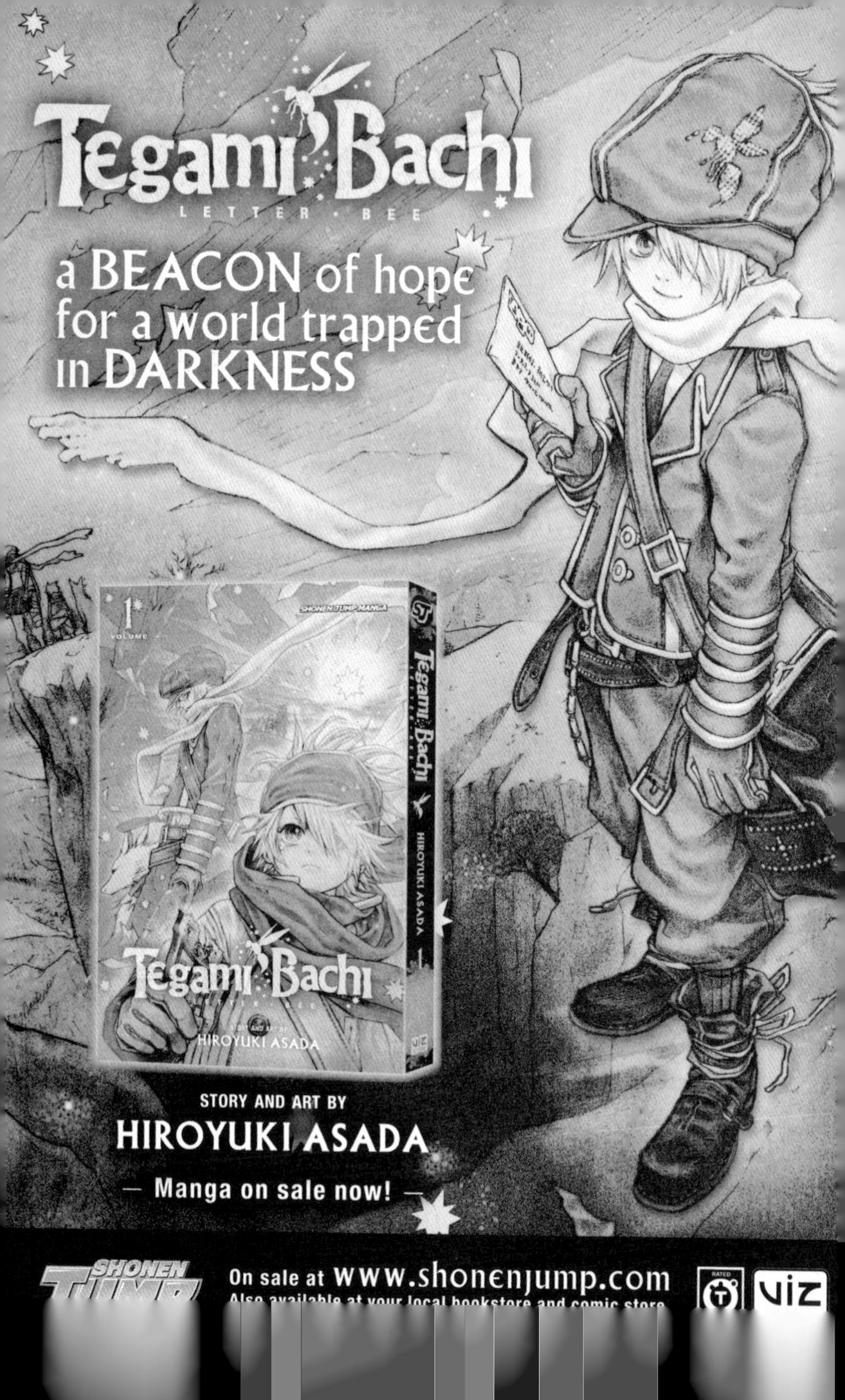

RATED
T
TEEN
ratings.viz.com

VIZ media

SJ
HIKARU no GO™
Manga on sale now!
$7.95
SHONEN JUMP GRAPHIC NOVEL
Yumi Hotta
Takeshi Obata
volume 1
An ancient ghost possesses Hikaru and unleashes his hidden genius!
SHONEN JUMP MANGA
HIKARU-NO GO © 1998 by Yumi Hotta, Takeshi Obata/SHUEISHA
On sale at:
www.shonenjump.com
Also available at your local bookstore and comic store.
RATED A FOR ALL AGES

You're Reading in the Wrong Direction!!

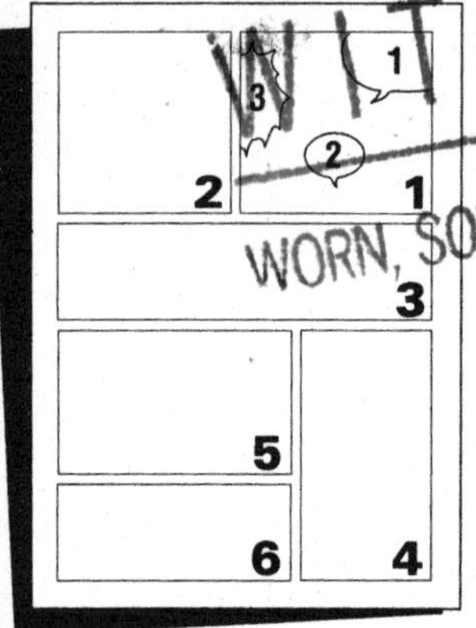
1
2
3
1
2
3
4
5
6

Whoops! Guess what? You're starting at the wrong end of the comic!

...It's true! In keeping with the original Japanese format, **Slam Dunk** is meant to be read from right to left, starting in the upper-right corner.

Unlike English, which is read from left to right, Japanese is read from right to left, meaning that action, sound effects and word-balloon order are completely reversed... something which can make readers unfamiliar with Japanese feel pretty backwards themselves. For this reason, manga or Japanese comics published in the U.S. in English have sometimes been published "flopped"—that is, printed in exact reverse order, as though seen from the other side of a mirror.

By flopping pages, U.S. publishers can avoid confusing readers, but the compromise is not without its downside. For one thing, a character in a flopped manga series who once wore in the original Japanese version a T-shirt emblazoned with "M A Y" (as in "the merry month of") now wears one which reads "Y A M"! Additionally, many manga creators in Japan are themselves unhappy with the process, as some feel the mirror-imaging of their art alters their original intentions.

We are proud to bring you Takehiko Inoue's **Slam Dunk** in the original unflopped format. For now, though, turn to the other side of the book and let the quest begin...!

–Editor